The Ultimate
Macro Diet Cookbook
for Beginners

1000-Day Easy & Healthy Recipes and 4 Weeks Meal Plan to Help You Burn Fat Quickly

Michele Pham

Contents

What is the Macro Diet?

The macro diet has grown in popularity in recent years. The diet allows people to consume any foods that meet their daily macronutrient ("macro") requirements. Rather than focusing solely on calories, there is an emphasis on counting and tracking macronutrients. Some diet supporters believe that adjusting macronutrient intake can help people lose weight and achieve their health and fitness goals.

What Exactly are Macros?

Macros, also known as macronutrients, provide energy to the body. People eat foods that contain three macronutrients—protein, fat, and carbohydrate. These macronutrients are found in varying amounts in various foods. We need to consume macronutrients in relatively large amounts because they provide energy to our bodies and help with multiple bodily functions.

Carbohydrates

Carbohydrates are the body's primary energy source. Before being absorbed into the blood, they are broken down into glucose (sugar). We need carbohydrates for the nervous system, kidneys, brain, and muscles to function properly. Carbohydrates can be found in various starchy foods, including bread, rice, potatoes, pasta, and breakfast cereals.

High-fiber starchy carbohydrates, such as wholegrain varieties, release glucose into the blood more slowly than high-sugar foods and drinks. Fiber is essential for overall health and lowers the risk of certain diseases such as bowel cancer, heart disease, and type 2 diabetes. It also aids in the promotion of digestive health.

Carbohydrates contain four calories per 1 gram. The Dietary Guidelines for Americans (DGA) recommends that adults consume 45%–65% of their daily calories from carbohydrates. Carbohydrate energy is critical for fueling the body and brain. However, the amount of carbohydrates required by each individual varies. Some people thrive on low-carb diets, while others require higher-carb ones.

Protein

The body requires proteins for tissue building and repair, cellular communication, enzymatic reactions, immune function, and other functions.

Protein-rich foods include meat, fish, eggs, beans, tofu, and nuts. One gram of protein contains approximately four calories. According to the DGA, adults should get 10%–35% of their daily calories from protein.

Fat

Fat aids in the storage of energy in the body. It also protects the nerves, regulates hormones, aids nutrient absorption, and keeps the body temperature stable. Fat is essential for a healthy body and mind.

Butter, oil, avocado, nuts, fatty fish, and meat are examples of high-fat foods. One gram of fat contains nine calories. According to the DGA, adults should consume 20%–35% of their daily calories from fat.

Some fats may be preferable to others (unsaturated fats over saturated fats). Fats are required for the normal structure of cells in the body. They also contain fat-soluble vitamins such as A, D, E, and K.

How to Count Macros: The Steps

Step 1: Determine your calorie requirements

You can estimate your daily calorie needs by using information about your body (such as age, height, and weight) and lifestyle through online or app calculators. Another option is using a formula, such as the Mifflin-St Jeor equation:

- Calories per day for men = 10 x weight (kg) + 6.25 x height (cm) – 5 x age (y) + 5
- Calories per day for women = 10 x weight (kg) + 6.25 x height (cm) – 5 x age (y) – 161

You then multiply the result by an activity factor, a number that represents your daily activity level:

- x 1.2 = sedentary (little or no exercise; desk job)
- x 1.375 = light active (light exercise one to three days a week)
- x 1.55 = moderately active (moderate exercise six to seven days a week)
- x 1.725 = very active (hard exercise every day or exercise twice a day)

- x 1.9 = extra active (difficult exercise more than two times a day)

The final figure represents your total daily energy expenditure (TDEE). This figure is the total amount of calories you require per day. People who want to lose or gain weight can slightly increase or decrease their calorie intake, but they should do so gradually.

Step 2: Calculate the macronutrient ratio

After calculating your total daily calorie requirements, you can calculate your macronutrient ratio.

The DGA suggests the following ratio:

- Proteins account for 10%–35% of total calories.
- Fats account for 20%–35% of total calories.
- Carbohydrates account for 45%–65% of total calories.

But this ratio changes in different disease-based diet plans.

Step 3: Keep track of macros

After determining your macronutrient ratio, you then need to track your food intake. You'll need to keep a food diary and pay close attention to the macronutrients you consume. Remember that macro tracking takes time. Rather than when tracking calories, following a macro diet requires you to pay close attention to the macronutrient ratio of everything you eat.

The Benefits of a Macro Diet

- Achieving weight loss objectives
- Gaining athletic performance benefits from lean muscle mass
- Controlling blood sugar levels
- Achieving and maintaining a physically healthier state overall

The most significant advantage of a macro diet is the freedom to eat foods you truly enjoy—as long as they fit your macro plan. Finding a good balance of nutrient-dense foods is essential. Choosing a macros plan that allows you to indulge on occasion makes it easier to stick to it in the long run.

If you want to lose weight, counting macros has one significant advantage—you'll consume slightly more protein than the average eater. The registered dietician and author of *The Protein Diet,* Georgie Fear, explains, "Protein requires more energy to digest and use than carbs or fat, and it suppresses your appetite." Macro diets force you to consider the quality of your food, influencing you to make more nutritious choices.

Banana Egg Pancakes

Preparation Time: 3 minutes
Cooking Time: 7 minutes
Serves: 1

Ingredients:

- 1 banana
- 2 eggs
- ½ tsp. coconut oil (or butter) for frying

Preparation:

1. Mash up the bananas in a large bowl.
2. Whisk the eggs (using a fork is just fine!) and add to the banana paste.
3. Fry the mixture gently in a pan on low-medium heat with a little heated oil or butter.

Serving Suggestion: Serve with maple syrup, yogurt, cherries, strawberries, honey, or cream.

Variation Tip: You can add some chopped nuts on top.

Nutritional Information per Serving:

Calories 241kcal | Protein 12g | Carbohydrates 28g | Fiber 3g | Sugars 15g | Fat 10g | Sodium 0.12◦

Egg Muffin

Preparation Time: 10 minutes
Cooking Time: 20 minutes
Serves: 3

Ingredients:

6 eggs
2 scallions, finely chopped
8 tbsp. peas (frozen is fine)
1 medium carrot, grated
3 tbsp. sesame seeds
3 tbsp. soy sauce
1 inch of ginger, grated
½ tsp. salt
1 tsp. olive oil

Preparation:

1. Preheat the oven to 390°F.
2. In a large mixing bowl, thoroughly combine the scallions, carrots, ginger, peas, sesame seeds, soy sauce, salt, and eggs.
3. Place the mixture in greased muffin tins and bake for 20 minutes.

Serving Suggestion: Serve with sweet chili sauce.

Variation Tip: Black pepper or any other spice can be added to the mixture before baking.

Nutritional Information per Serving:

Calories 340kcal | Fat 14g | Sodium 1.53g | Carbohydrates 12g | Fiber 4g | Sugars 4g | Protein 17g

Chickpea Flour Pancakes

Preparation Time: 5 minutes
Cooking Time: 5 minutes
Serves: 4

Ingredients:

- 1 cup chickpea flour (or besan/garbanzo flour)
- 1 cup water
- 1 tsp. turmeric
- ½ tsp. salt
- ½ tsp. pepper
- 3 scallions, finely diced
- 1 tbsp. olive oil (or ghee)

Optional

- ½ tsp. chili flakes (I highly recommend this)
- 1 red bell pepper, finely diced
- ½ cup peas

Preparation:

1. In a mixing bowl, combine the flour, water, turmeric, salt, pepper, and chili flakes (if using) an pulse or blend until smooth. The batter should be extremely runny!
2. Allow the mixture to rest for a few minutes while you prepare the oil or ghee in a non-stick par Ensure that the bottom of the pan is well coated and heat on a medium heat.
3. Toss the diced bell pepper and scallions into the batter mixture.
4. When the pan is heated, add approximately a ladleful of the mixture to it.
5. Cook for approximately 3 minutes, or until the mixture begins to thicken up. You can create tw pancakes at the same time if you use two pans.
6. If you want thin pancakes, make sure you use a big skillet (or pans). They're a LOT simpler to wor with!
7. Flip the pancakes with a big spatula, adding additional oil below if required. Your pancake will b done in about 2 to 3 minutes!
8. Place the pancake somewhere warm while you make the second one, using additional oil as needed
9. It's all done! Enjoy with your favorite toppings. Remember to eat these pancakes while they're sti warm—don't let them cool!

Serving Suggestion: These pancakes can be served with any chutney or yogurt.

Variation Tip: Olive oil can be replaced with any other oil or butter.

Nutritional Information per Serving:
Calories 253kcal | Protein 10.1g | Carbohydrates 33g | Fiber 9.4g | Sugars 6.4g | Fat 10g | Sodiur 0.30g

Omelet

Preparation Time: 2 minutes
Cooking Time: 8 minutes
Serves: 1

Ingredients:

- 2 eggs
- 1 tsp. olive oil
- ½ cup cherry tomatoes (the sweeter, the better), finely chopped
- ½ cup fresh basil (dried will work if necessary)
- ¼ cup your favorite cheese (think cheddar, Monterey Jack, mozzarella. Remember to avoid rennet if you're vegetarian)
- Salt and pepper to taste

Optional

- 2 scallions, finely chopped
- 1 chili pepper (red or green), finely chopped

Preparation:

1. In a skillet, heat half of the oil and cook the tomatoes for 2 minutes. Remove from the skillet. Using a paper towel, wipe the pan clean.
2. In a mixing dish, crack the eggs and beat them thoroughly with a fork, seasoning with the salt and pepper.
3. In a pan (non-stick if possible), heat the remaining oil on low to medium heat. Wipe the oil around a little with a paper towel (or use an oil spray if you have it).
4. Fill the pan with the egg mixture.
5. Ruffle the omelet using a spatula to prevent it from sticking. As you make gaps, tilt the pan to allow the liquid to fill them.
6. Allow it to simmer for around 2 minutes. The next crucial step is to add the tomatoes and basil (along with any cheese, scallions, or chili if you're using them). Do this when the egg mixture appears nearly done (but there's still a small amount of runny egg remaining).
7. Fold the omelet's empty half on top of the other.
8. Close the omelet and slide it onto a dish; the heat from the closed omelet will finish cooking the interior.

Serving Suggestion: Serve with fresh bread.

Variation Tip: Sprinkle some spices into the mixture before cooking.

Nutritional Information per Serving:
Calories 145kcal | Protein 4.9g | Carbohydrates 13.6g | Fiber 1.7g | Sugars 6.7g | Fat 11.6g | Sodium 0.05g

Egg With Avocado Bread

Preparation Time: 3 minutes
Cooking Time: 5 minutes
Serves: 1

Ingredients:

- 1 slice of bread
- ½ medium avocado, mashed
- 1 tsp. lemon juice
- 1 egg
- ½ tsp. olive oil
- Salt and pepper to taste

Preparation:

1. Fry the egg in the olive oil in a pan over medium heat. Meanwhile, toast the bread in a toaster.
2. Season the mashed avocado with salt and pepper and the lemon juice.
3. Spread the mashed avocado over the toasted bread.
4. When the egg has fried to your liking, place it on top of the mashed avocado on toast.

Serving Suggestion: Serve with your favorite spicy sauce—Sriracha works really well!

Variation Tip: Add a little more oil to the pan and toast your bread next to the egg.

Nutritional Information per Serving:
Calories 312kcal | Carbohydrates 21g | Protein 11g | Fat 22g | Sodium 1.34g | Fiber 9g | Sugar 3g

Breakfast Potatoes

Preparation Time: 15 minutes
Cooking Time: 15 minutes
Serves: 2

Ingredients:

- 2 tbsp. olive oil
- 3 medium potatoes (roughly 14 oz.), cubed (about the size of your little finger)
- 2 medium onions, peeled and sliced into half rings
- 7 oz. firm tofu
- 1 tsp. cumin
- 2 tsp. oregano, dried
- 1 tsp. salt
- 1 tsp. black pepper
- ½ cup cherry tomatoes, halved

Preparation:

1. Set a small amount of the olive oil in a pan over low-medium heat. Add the potatoes and cook them, stirring gently, for 5 minutes. Add the onions when the potatoes begin to sweat.
2. Crumble in the tofu. Add the spices, salt, and pepper and stir to combine. Cover the pan with a lid and cook for 15 minutes. If you think more oil is required, you may add it—or replace it with a bit of hot water to conserve calories.
3. Add a drop of olive oil to a second pan and wipe it around using a paper towel. Heat the pan over medium heat. Add the tomatoes and cook until some black spots emerge (about 5 minutes). If you like, add a few drops of boiling water to help the tomatoes cook. Add salt and pepper to taste.
4. If you don't have a second pan or don't want to use another one, place the potatoes on a platter and cover (or keep warm in a preheated oven).
5. Arrange the tomato and potato mixture on a platter. It's done!

Serving Suggestion: Add spices of your choice.

Variation Tip: You can either peel the potatoes or leave the skin on.

Nutritional Information per Serving:
Calories 423kcal | Fat 19g | Sodium 1.19g | Carbohydrates 51g | Fiber 9g | Sugars 8g | Protein 15g

Avocado Sandwich

Preparation Time: 5 minutes
Cooking Time: 5 minutes
Serves: 1

Ingredients:

- 2 slices bread (whole wheat)
- 3 to 4 slices of your favorite cheese (just check that it uses vegetarian rennet)
- ½ avocado (the other half can be used in a smoothie or guacamole), sliced
- 4 to 6 dried cranberries, halved
- ½ small tomato (the other half could also be used in guacamole), sliced
- 1 small handful of arugula
- ½ tbsp. balsamic vinegar

Preparation:

1. Combine all of the Ingredients on one slice of bread and sprinkle with balsamic vinegar.
2. Simply place the second slice of bread on top of the sandwich to "close" it. Squish it a little to keep any parts from slipping out.

Serving Suggestion: Serve with homemade mayonnaise.

Variation Tip: Spread the bread slices with cream cheese before adding the avocado mixture.

Nutritional Information per Serving:

Calories 405kcal | Carbohydrates 33g | Fiber 9g | Sugar 6g | Protein 16g | Fat 25g | Sodium 0.56g

Tomato Mozzarella Bread

Preparation Time: 5 minutes
Cooking Time: 5 minutes
Serves: 2

Ingredients:

- ½ cup cherry tomatoes, halved
- 1 ball low-fat mozzarella cheese (4.5 oz.), thinly sliced
- ¼ cup fresh basil, chopped
- 1 tbsp. olive oil
- 1 tbsp. balsamic vinegar
- Salt and pepper to taste
- 2 to 3 slices of bread (whole wheat or rustic/farm bread)

Preparation:

1. Preheat the oven to 360°F.
2. Apply a thin layer of olive oil onto the bread slices.
3. Layer the mozzarella and then the tomatoes on top of the bread slices.
4. Season the chopped basil with the salt and pepper and place it on top.
5. Place the bread in the oven for about 5 minutes or until golden brown, and the cheese has melted.
6. Eat the bread when it is still warm.

Serving Suggestion: Put the vinegar on last for a fuller flavor.

Variation Tip: Use another low-fat cheese if you prefer.

Nutritional Information per Serving:

Calories 304kcal | Fat 18g | Sodium 0.50g | Carbohydrates 16g | Fiber 2g | Sugar 4g | Protein 19g

Tempeh Sandwich

Preparation Time: 7 minutes
Cooking Time: 3 minutes
Serves: 2

Ingredients:

- 4 slices whole-wheat bread
- 3 oz. tempeh (in 8 slices)
- 2 handfuls arugula
- ½ cup sun-dried tomatoes in oil, drained and chopped
- 1 tbsp. olive oil
- 2 tbsp. vinegar (balsamic, malt, or wine vinegar)
- 2 tbsp. soy sauce
- 2 tsp. maple syrup
- 1 avocado
- ½ lemon (juiced)
- Salt and pepper to taste

Preparation:

1. Fry the tempeh slices over medium heat in the olive oil.
2. Add the soy sauce, vinegar, and maple syrup after a few minutes. Cook for another 3 to 4 minutes, stirring occasionally.
3. Remove the avocado flesh and place it in a bowl with the lemon juice, salt, and pepper. Mi everything together well.
4. Cover two of the bread slices with the avocado mixture.
5. Arrange the arugula over the other two slices. Add the chopped dried tomatoes.
6. Place the cooked tempeh on bread slices covered with the arugula.
7. Make two sandwiches by placing the avocado-covered slices on top of the other two.

Serving Suggestion: You can add spices of your choice.

Variation Tip: You can also fry the sandwich in a little oil after it has been assembled.

Nutritional Information per Serving:
Calories 547kcal | Fat 37g | Sodium 2.48g | Carbohydrates 41g | Fiber 13g | Sugars 9g | Protein 21

Scrambled Eggs With Cheese

Preparation Time: 2 minutes
Cooking Time: 3 minutes
Serves: 1

Ingredients:

2 eggs
¼ cup cheddar cheese (or Monterey Jack), grated
½ tsp. olive oil (or butter)
Salt and pepper to taste

Preparation:

1. Heat the butter or oil in a frying pan over medium heat.
2. Break the eggs into a bowl and rapidly whisk them together with a fork.
3. Season the egg mixture with salt and pepper.
4. Pour the beaten eggs into the frying pan.
5. Layer the grated cheese on top of the eggs.
6. The eggs will start to solidify almost immediately, so use a spatula to "pull" them in from the side to the center as soon as they do. Do this "pulling" several times.
7. It just takes a few minutes for the eggs to cook. They should be soft and gently cooked.
8. You're done when the egg has no more "watery" parts. Remove from the pan and place on a plate as soon as possible.

Serving Suggestion: Serve with fresh bread.

Variation Tip: Add some cayenne pepper to enhance the flavor.

Nutritional Information per Serving:
Calories 327kcal | Fat 21g | Sodium 0.87g | Carbohydrates 13g | Fiber 2g | Sugars 2g | Protein 22g

Pot Chicken Tenders

Preparation Time: 4 minutes
Cooking Time: 6 minutes
Serves: 4

Ingredients:

- 1 tsp. Italian seasoning
- ½ tsp. onion powder
- ¼ tsp. garlic powder
- ½ tsp. salt
- ¼ tsp. pepper
- 2 lb. chicken tenders
- 1 cup chicken broth

Preparation:

1. In a dish, season both sides of each chicken tender with the seasoning, onion and garlic powder, salt, and pepper.
2. Set the Instant Pot to sauté (or do this step on the stovetop) and brown the chicken tenders for 1 to 2 minutes on each side. This step is optional, but it helps to lock in the taste.
3. Place the chicken inside the Instant Pot and cover with the chicken broth.
4. Seal the pressure cooker and set it to cook on high for 6 minutes.
5. When the chicken is done, open the pressure valve and wait for the pressure to dissipate before allowing it to rest for another 5 minutes.

Serving Suggestion: Serve with a dipping sauce of your choice and enjoy!

Variation Tip: Browning the chicken tenders is optional.

Nutritional Information per Serving:
Calories 176kcal | Carbohydrates 1g | Protein 32g | Fat 4g | Sodium 0.51g | Fiber 1g | Sugar 1g

Grilled Chicken Breast

Preparation Time: 5 minutes
Cooking Time: 15 minutes
Serves: 4

Ingredients:

- ½ tsp. salt
- ¼ tsp. pepper
- ½ tsp. cumin
- 1 tsp. chili powder
- ½ tsp. onion powder
- ¼ tsp. garlic powder
- 2 tbsp. olive oil
- 2 lb. boneless, skinless chicken breasts
- Fresh lime juice
- Handful fresh cilantro, chopped

Preparation:

1. Heat up a large griddle pan on a medium-high heat.
2. Combine the salt, pepper, cumin, chili powder, onion powder, and garlic powder in a small dish. Drizzle the olive oil over the chicken breasts and then massage the spice mixture all over them.
3. Place the chicken breasts on the heated griddle pan and cook for about 15 minutes total, turning halfway through. Squeeze fresh lime juice over the chicken and sprinkle with the cilantro before serving.

Serving Suggestion: Serve with tortilla wraps.

Variation Tip: Add spices of your choice.

Nutritional Information per Serving:
Calories 374kcal | Carbohydrates 1g | Protein 44g| Fat 16g | Sodium 0.50g | Fiber 1g | Sugar 1g

Creamy Garlic Chicken

Preparation Time: 10 minutes
Cooking Time: 20 minutes
Serves: 4

Ingredients:

- 4 small chicken breasts (or 2 large) cut in half, lengthwise
- ¼ cup all-purpose flour
- 1½ tbsp. unsalted butter, divided
- 1 tbsp. olive oil
- 1 head of garlic, peeled
- ½ cup dry white wine
- 1 cup heavy cream
- 2 cups packed baby spinach

Preparation:

1. Season both sides of the chicken breasts with salt and pepper.
2. On a medium plate, sprinkle the flour. Dredge each segment of chicken breast in the flour and pat off any excess.
3. In a large skillet with high sides, heat 1 tablespoon of the butter and all the olive oil on a medium high heat. Add the chicken breasts when the butter has melted.
4. Sear the chicken on one side for 3 to 4 minutes, or until golden brown. Cook for another 2 to 3 minutes on the other side until brown. Place the chicken breasts on a plate. (Don't worry about the chicken being fully cooked; it will continue cooking later.)
5. In the same pan, melt the remaining amount of butter. Reduce the heat to medium-low and toss in all of the peeled garlic cloves. Toast the garlic cloves until they are golden brown on all sides. Take caution not to overheat the garlic.
6. Pour the wine in. Bring to a boil, then lower to a low heat. Simmer until the liquid has been reduced by half.
7. Pour in the cream once the wine has reduced. Bring the cream and wine back to a boil, then reduce to a low heat.
8. Return the chicken to the sauce, cover, and simmer until the chicken is well cooked and the internal temperature reaches 165°F.
9. Add the spinach once the chicken has finished cooking. Close the cover and continue to cook for another 1 to 2 minutes.
10. Remove the cover and mix the spinach, chicken, and sauce together until the spinach has thoroughly wilted, seasoning with salt and pepper to taste.

Serving Suggestion: Serve with a tortilla and enjoy!

Variation Tip: Add pepperoni, mushrooms, and olives to give it extra flavor.

Nutritional Information per Serving:
Calories 531kcal | Carbohydrates 9g | Protein 51g | Fat 31g | Sodium 0.29g | Fiber 1g | Sugar 1g

Lemon Butter Chicken

Preparation Time: 5 minutes
Cooking Time: 45 minutes
Serves: 4

Ingredients:

- 4 chicken thighs, bone-in, skin-on
- 1 tsp. kosher salt (plus more to taste)
- 1 tsp. lemon pepper
- 3 tbsp. salted butter, divided
- 3 cloves garlic, minced (or 1½ tsp. garlic paste)
- ½ cup low-sodium chicken broth
- 1 cup heavy cream
- ½ cup parmesan cheese, grated
- ¼ cup fresh lemon juice
- 1 tsp. fresh thyme leaves plus more for garnish
- 5 oz. baby spinach

Preparation:

1. Preheat the oven to 400°F.
2. In a mixing dish, combine the chicken thighs with the salt and lemon pepper. Toss everything together.
3. Preheat an oven-safe medium/large skillet over medium-high heat. Allow 2 tablespoons of butter to melt in the skillet, making sure the entire bottom is covered.
4. Sear the chicken, skin side down, for 3 to 4 minutes, or until golden brown. Flip it over and sear the other side. Remove the chicken from the pan and put it aside.
5. Return the skillet to the heat and add 1 tablespoon more of butter. Allow the butter to melt in the pan while stirring and deglazing it.
6. Cook the garlic for 1 to 2 minutes in the skillet until it is aromatic.
7. Combine the chicken broth, heavy cream, parmesan cheese, lemon juice, and thyme in a mixing bowl. Stir everything together, so they completely mix.
8. Add the broth mixture to the skillet, bring to a boil, then lower to a low heat.
9. Allow 5 minutes for the sauce to thicken before adding the spinach leaves.
10. Stir to wilt the leaves gently, but not to cook completely.
11. Return the chicken to the skillet and place it in the oven. Bake for 25 minutes, or until the internal temperature of the chicken reaches 165°F.

Serving Suggestion: Serve alone or with tortilla wraps, rice, spaghetti, or mashed potatoes. Add a few lemon slices and fresh thyme as a garnish. Enjoy!

Variation Tip: Sprinkle with parmesan cheese before putting it in the oven.

Nutritional Information per Serving:
Calories 603kcal | Carbohydrates 6g | Protein 26g | Fat 53g | Sodium 0.09g | Fiber 1g | Sugar 1g

Parmesan Chicken Cutlets

Preparation Time: 10 minutes
Cooking Time: 40 minutes
Serves: 8

Ingredients:

- 4 boneless, skinless chicken breasts
- Kosher salt
- Freshly ground black pepper
- 3 large eggs, beaten
- 1 cup all-purpose flour
- 2¼ cup panko breadcrumbs
- ¾ cup parmesan cheese, freshly grated
- 2 tsp. lemon zest
- ½ tsp. cayenne pepper
- Vegetable oil

Preparation:

1. Cut the chicken breasts in half crosswise with a sharp knife. Place the halves on a chopping boar
between two pieces of plastic wrap. Flatten the chicken with a meat tenderizer or a rolling pin to
thickness of 14 inches. Season both sides of the chicken with salt and pepper.
2. Separate the eggs and flour into two small bowls. Combine the panko, parmesan, lemon zest, an
cayenne in a third shallow dish. Add salt to taste.
3. Working one at a time, coat the chicken cutlets in the flour, egg, and panko mixture, pressing t
adhere.
4. Heat 2 tablespoons of oil in a large pan over medium heat. Cook the cutlets for 2 to 3 minutes pe
side, or until golden and heated through. As required, work in batches, adding additional oil as needed

Serving Suggestion: Serve with lemon wedges.

Variation Tip: Sprinkle some onions and cheese to add more to its flavor.

Nutritional Information per Serving:
Calories 213kcal | Fat 9.9g | Sodium 0.32g | Carbohydrates 13g | Fiber 0.9g | Sugars 2g | Protein 17

Apricot Glazed Chicken

Preparation Time: 10 minutes
Cooking Time: 35-40 minutes
Serves: 6

Ingredients:

- 6 skinless, boneless chicken breasts
- 1 can (10.75 oz.) low-sodium chicken broth
- ¾ cup apricot preserve
- 1 tbsp. light soy sauce
- 1 tbsp. cornstarch
- 1 tbsp. water

Preparation:

1. Coat a large skillet with non-stick cooking spray. Heat the skillet on a medium heat.
2. In the hot skillet, brown the chicken.
3. Combine the chicken broth, preserve, and soy sauce in a mixing bowl. Add to the skillet and cook for 20 minutes, or until chicken is cooked through (no longer pink in the center).
4. Remove the chicken from the pan. To thicken the sauce, combine 1 tablespoon of cornstarch and 1 tablespoon of water (more of each in equal amounts if you like it thicker). Return the chicken to the skillet and turn to coat thoroughly with the sauce.

Serving Suggestion: Serve with rice if desired.

Variation Tip: You can substitute orange juice or marmalade for the apricot preserve to make orange-glazed chicken.

Nutritional Information per Serving:

Calories 296kcal | Fat 1.9g | Sodium 0.22g | Carbohydrates 35g | Sugars 1.3g | Fiber 0.95g | Protein 33.7g

Chicken Fried Rice

Preparation Time: 10 minutes
Cooking Time: 30 minutes
Serves: 1

Ingredients:

- 2 cups white rice (jasmine or basmati)
- 3 tbsp. plus 1 tsp. canola or vegetable oil, divided
- 1 boneless, skinless chicken breast
- 1 small yellow onion, diced
- 1 medium carrot, peeled and diced
- 3 scallions, thinly sliced diagonally
- 2 medium garlic cloves, minced
- 3 tsp. low-sodium soy sauce
- 2 tsp. toasted sesame oil

- kosher salt & freshly ground black pepper to taste
- 1 tbsp. mirin
- 1 cup frozen baby peas
- 2 large eggs, lightly beaten

Preparation:

1. Cook the rice according to the package directions, then transfer it to a dish to cool fully. Once the rice has fully cooled, break it up into individual grains with your fingertips.
2. In a 12-inch non-stick skillet (or wok), heat 1 tablespoon of oil over a high heat until it starts smoking.
3. Add the rice and simmer, stirring occasionally, for 3 to 4 minutes, or until the rice begins to darken slightly. Take the rice out, place it in a small mixing dish, and set it aside.
4. Turn the heat to medium, add 1 tablespoon of oil to the skillet, and add the chicken breasts. Cook each side for 3 minutes.
5. Transfer the chicken to a cutting board and slice it into very thin slices, then thirds.
6. Heat 1 tablespoon of oil in a pan and add the chopped onion, carrot, scallions, and garlic. Cook for 2 to 3 minutes, stirring constantly, or until the carrots are just barely cooked and the onions are transparent.
7. Stir in the rice and peas until everything is well combined.
8. Combine the cooked chicken, soy sauce, sesame oil, and mirin in a mixing bowl. Cook in the skillet for another 2 minutes.
9. Season with freshly ground black pepper and kosher salt to taste.
10. Push the chicken rice mixture to the sides of the skillet and pour 1 tablespoon of oil into the center.
11. Add the lightly beaten eggs and season with salt and pepper. Scramble the eggs and add them to the chicken/rice combination.
12. Cook everything for another 3 to 4 minutes, stirring often, to allow the flavors to blend.

Serving Suggestion: Serve the dish with a dash of chili sauce.

Variation Tip: Add some chopped chilis to the chicken as it is cooking to add some spice.

Nutritional Information per Serving:
Calories 337kcal | Fat 16g | Sodium 0.24g | Carbohydrates 35g | Fiber 2.8g | Sugars 5g | Protein 14g

Honey Sesame Chicken

Preparation Time: 10 minutes
Cooking Time: 30 minutes
Serves: 4

Ingredients:
For the chicken:
- 3 chicken breasts (about 1 lb.)
- 2 eggs
- 1½ tbsp. soy sauce
- 2½ tbsp. coconut flour (or regular flour)
- ½ cup cold water
- ½ tbsp. coconut oil

For the sauce:
- ⅓ cup honey
- 1 tbsp. tomato sauce
- 1 tsp. ground ginger
- 1 tsp. garlic powder
- ¼ tsp. chili powder
- 1 tsp. apple cider vinegar
- 3 tbsp. sesame oil
- 1 tbsp. lemon juice
- ½ tsp. salt
- 1 tbsp. coconut flour (or regular flour)
- ⅓ cup water
- 2 tbsp. sesame seeds

Preparation:
For the chicken:
1. Cut the chicken breasts into little bite-size pieces.
2. In a large mixing bowl, whisk together the eggs.
3. Pour in the soy sauce and water.
4. Mix in the coconut flour thoroughly until no lumps remain.
5. Add the chicken to the bowl and mix thoroughly. Allow it to sit for 10 minutes.
6. Add the coconut oil to a non-stick frying pan and melt over medium heat.
7. Toss the chicken into the frying pan using tongs and cook for 4 minutes on each side or until golden brown. Place each piece on a cooling rack or paper towel after each side has been cooked. Depending on how little your chicken bites are, you may need to repeat this process. When you're cooking the chicken, be sure the pieces aren't touching.
8. Add the sesame oil to the leftover coconut oil once you've taken the last batch from the pan. While making the honey glaze, combine all the chicken pieces and fry for 10 minutes on medium heat. Stir often.

For the honey glaze:
1. Combine the honey, tomato sauce, ginger, garlic, chili, apple cider vinegar, lemon juice, salt, and coconut flour in a small saucepan. Mix thoroughly, ensuring no lumps remain.
2. Put the saucepan on a low heat and bring to a gentle simmer before adding the water.
3. Cook over medium-high heat for 8 minutes or until the sauce has slightly thickened.
4. Pour it over the chicken, toss in the sesame seeds, and serve!

Serving Suggestion: Serve with a tortilla.
Variation Tip: Add spices of your choice to the glaze.
Nutritional Information per Serving:
Calories 504kcal | Carbohydrates 29g | Sugars 24g | Sodium 0.93g | Fat 24g | Protein 41g | Fiber 2g

Chicken Enchiladas

Preparation Time: 10 minutes
Cooking Time: 40 minutes
Serves: 6

Ingredients:

- 2 tbsp. butter
- 2 tbsp. flour
- 1 can (10 oz.) red enchilada sauce
- 1 cup chicken broth
- 1 tbsp. canola oil
- 2 yellow onions, diced
- 4 oz. can diced green chiles
- 3 cups rotisserie chicken, shredded (about ½ rotisserie chicken)
- 1 tbsp. cumin
- 1 tsp. chili powder
- ½ tsp. kosher salt
- ½ tsp. freshly ground black pepper
- 6 oz. queso fresco, crumbled
- 1 cup sour cream
- 16 oz. Monterey Jack cheese, shredded and divided
- 8 large flour tortillas
- ¼ cup cilantro, chopped

Preparation:

1. Preheat the oven to 350°F.
2. Melt the butter in a small saucepan over medium heat, then add the flour. Cook while continuall stirring.
3. Stir in the enchilada sauce, broth, salt, and pepper. Bring to a boil, then lower to a low heat an continue to cook, stirring periodically, while you prepare the remaining Ingredients.
4. Heat the oil in a large pan until it shimmers. Cook the onion, stirring occasionally, for 5 to 7 minutes or until the onions are transparent.
5. Combine the chicken with the diced green chilies, cumin, and chili powder and add to the pan.
6. Remove the pan from the heat and stir in 2 cups of the shredded cheese along with the sour crean and queso fresco. Stir until the cheese has melted and everything is thoroughly mixed.
7. Remove the enchilada sauce from the heat. Spread a ½ cup of the sauce over the bottom of a larg baking dish.
8. Fill 1 tortilla with 1/3 cup of the chicken filling, roll firmly, and set seam-side down in the bakin dish.
9. Continue with the remaining tortillas.
10. Pour the remaining sauce over the wrapped tortillas and top with the remaining Monterey Jac cheese.
11. Bake for 25 to 30 minutes, or until the cheese is completely melted and bubbling. Remove fron oven and set aside for 5 minutes to cool.

Serving Suggestion: Serve with chopped cilantro on top.

Variation Tip: Add granulated cilantro to the filling for extra flavor.

Nutritional Information per Serving:

Calories 773kcal | Protein 45g | Carbohydrates 34g | Fiber 3g | Sugars 9g | Fat 51g | Sodium 1.98g

Mexican Chicken Soup

Preparation Time: 10 minutes
Cooking Time: 2 hours
Serves: 5

Ingredients:

   1 lb. chicken pieces (bone-in legs, thighs, breasts)
   4 tbsp. olive oil
   1 onion, finely chopped
   2 garlic cloves, crushed
   1 tsp. ground cumin
   1 tsp. ground chili powder
   1 tsp. dried oregano
   1 tsp. paprika
   10 cups water
   1 large carrot, sliced
   1 can (10 oz.) red enchilada sauce
   1 can diced tomatoes
   1 tsp. salt
   ½ tsp. black ground pepper
   ⅓ cup brown rice
   1 jalapeno, sliced
   1 avocado, sliced
   Juice of 3 limes

Preparation:

1. Pour the olive oil into a large saucepan and heat over a medium heat.
2. Combine the onion, garlic, chili powder, cumin, paprika, and dried oregano in a large mixing bowl.
3. Add the mixture to the heated saucepan and cook for 7 minutes or until golden brown.
4. Add the water, chicken, carrot slices, chopped tomato, enchilada sauce, salt, and pepper.
5. Bring to a boil, then reduce to a low heat and continue to cook for 2 hours.
6. Remove the chicken from the broth and shred it. Return the chicken to the soup.
7. Cook for another 35 to 40 minutes with the brown rice.
8. Remove the pan from the heat and stir in the sliced jalapenos, avocado, and lime juice.

Serving Suggestion: Garnish with sour cream, cilantro, and shredded cheese.

Variation Tip: Add spices of your choice to the mixture while cooking.

Nutritional Information per Serving:
Calories 492kcal | Protein 17g | Carbohydrates 34g | Fiber 8g | Sugars 10g | Fat 32g |Sodium 1.56g

White Miso Black Cod

Preparation Time: 1 hour
Cooking Time: 20 minutes
Serves: 4

Ingredients:

- 4 x 4 oz. pieces of black cod

For the miso marinade:

- 3 tbsp. mirin
- 3 tbsp. sake
- 1/3 cup white miso paste
- 1/3 cup sugar

Preparation:

1. Preheat the oven to 400°F.
2. Bring the mirin and sake to a boil in a small saucepan. Whisk in the miso until it is completely dissolved.
3. Add the sugar and cook, whisking constantly, until it is completely dissolved. Transfer the marinade to a large baking dish and set it aside to cool.
4. Turn the fish in the marinade to coat it. Cover and refrigerate overnight or for at least 1 to 2 hours. The longer, the better.
5. In a heavy bottom skillet, heat a little oil over medium-high heat. Remove the marinade from the fish but don't rinse it off. Place the fish, skin side up, in the skillet, and sear for 2 to 3 minutes, or until brown and caramelized. Turn the fish over and cook for another 2 to 3 minutes to crisp it up.
6. Finish the fish by roasting it in the oven for 8 to 10 minutes, or until flaky.

Serving Suggestion: Serve the fish with rice and veggies in a bowl

Variation Tip: Add spices of your choice.

Nutritional Information per Serving:

Calories 228kcal | Fat 3g | Sodium 0.63g | Carbohydrates 15.1g | Sugars 2g | Protein 30g | Fiber 0g

Lobster Bisque

Preparation Time: 20 minutes
Cooking Time: 30 minutes
Serves: 3

Ingredients:

4 to 5 lobster tails (4 to 6 oz. each) or 20 oz. total
5 cups water
1 tsp. salt
2 tbsp. olive oil or ghee
1 onion, diced
2 fat garlic cloves, roughly chopped
2 stalks (1 cup) celery, diced
½ tsp. dried thyme or 1 tsp. fresh thyme
1 medium yam (2 cups), peeled and diced (or carrots)
2 tbsp. tomato paste
½ tsp. sweet paprika
1 bay leaf
½ cup sherry wine or white wine (do not use sherry vinegar)
3 cups lobster stock (you'll make this with the shells from the lobster) or see notes
1 cup heavy cream (or coconut milk)

Optional:

- Fish sauce
- Salt
- Pepper
- Cayenne pepper
- 1 to 2 tbsp. butter
- 2 garlic cloves, smashed

For the garnish: tarragon, chives, or flatleaf parsley (tarragon is classic for this dish).

Preparation:

1. Prepare the lobster and stock: Combine the lobster tails, 5 cups of water, and 1 teaspoon of salt in a stockpot. Bring to a boil, then reduce to a low heat and cook for 5 to 7 minutes, or until the tails are bright red and curling. Using tongs, place the tails in a dish, keeping the hot lobster water in the saucepan.

2. Remove the flesh from the lobster tails and return the shells to the lobster water together with any liquid. Cook for 20 minutes while you finish preparing the remainder of the soup. Chop the lobster flesh into small pieces, leaving a few bigger red bits for garnishing. Any red roe, which will add taste and color, should be kept. Refrigerate.

3. Heat the oil in a heavy-bottomed pot or Dutch oven over medium-high heat for the bisque. Sauté the onion for 3 to 4 minutes, or until aromatic. Reduce heat to medium, add the garlic, celery, and thyme, and cook for another 5 minutes until the onions are cooked. Cook for 2 minutes before adding the diced yam, tomato paste, paprika, and bay leaf. Stir for 1 to 2 minutes. Deglaze with the sherry, scraping off any browned pieces, and finish cooking, or if you prefer, carefully tilt the pot to let it ignite (stand back!) and burn off the alcohol.

4. The lobster stock should be strained (around 3 cups should be enough). Combine this with the vegetables in the saucepan. Cook until the yam and celery are soft, approximately 15 minutes, over medium-low heat, covered. The bay leaf should be removed.

5. A quarter of the chopped lobster should be added to this, and everything should be smooth and creamy (either use an immersion blender or blend in batches using a regular blender).

6. Return this to the Dutch oven. Pour in the cream. Taste and add as much salt and pepper as necessary. A small drop of fish sauce may assist in creating depth. A pinch or two of cayenne pepper is excellent if you want a little kick.

7. Swirl the butter and crushed garlic cloves in a medium pan over medium-high heat until nutty and fragrant. Sauté for another 1 to 2 minutes with the leftover lobster. Set aside a few of the largest and most beautiful pieces for garnish, and add the rest of the smaller pieces to the soup. Continue to cook the soup on low heat for a few more minutes. After the flavors have had time to mingle, it will taste more "lobstery." I'll sometimes leave it on the stove for half an hour before gently reheating it before serving.

8. Divide among dishes and top with the larger lobster pieces and fresh tarragon.

Serving Suggestion: Serve with warm garlic bread.

Variation Tip: Add spices of your choice.

Nutritional Information per Serving:

Calories 514kcal | Protein 40g | Carbohydrates 26g | Fiber 4.4g | Sugars 4.9g | Fat 25g | Sodium 1.36g

Portuguese Fish Stew

Preparation Time: 20 minutes

Cooking Time: 30 minutes

Serves: 4

Ingredients:

- 3 tbsp. olive oil
- 1 onion, diced
- 4 garlic cloves, roughly chopped
- 2 tomatoes, diced
- ¼ cup white wine
- 4 cups chicken stock (or fish stock)
- 2 tsp. fish sauce (skip if using fish stock)
- Large pinch saffron, crumbled
- ⅛ tsp. ground clove (or allspice)—optional
- ¼ tsp. smoked paprika
- ¼ tsp. salt
- ¼ tsp. pepper
- 2 bay leaves
- 1 to 2 tbsp. fresh thyme (lemon thyme also works well)
- 1 lb. potatoes, cut into 1-inch cubes (Yukon, baby red or white. Keeping on thin skins is okay, bu you should peel russets).
- 1.5 lb. fish fillets, boneless and skinless (use wild cod, haddock, sea bass, salmon—or feel free t mix in or substitute shellfish, such as clams, mussels, shrimp, etc.), cut into 1½ -inch pieces.

Preparation:

1. Heat the oil in a large Dutch oven or heavy-bottom pot over medium heat. Add the onion and garlic Cook while stirring until they are aromatic and golden (about 6 minutes).
2. Toss in the tomatoes, along with their juices. Cook the tomatoes for about 4 minutes, or until the have softened.
3. Add the white wine and simmer for 2 to 3 minutes, or until most of the wine has evaporated.
4. Add the chicken broth, fish sauce, saffron, a pinch of ground clove or allspice (optional), smoke paprika, salt, pepper, bay leaves, and fresh thyme.
5. Bring to a boil with the potatoes. Cover the pot and cook on low heat for 15 minutes, or until th potatoes are fork-tender.
6. Add the fish, reducing the pot to a low simmer over medium heat, and give it a gentle toss. Do no overmix, or the fish will fall apart. Cook the fish until it is just cooked through (about 3 to 4 minutes Turn the heat off.
7. Take a sip of the broth. Add salt to taste.
8. Use freshly torn Italian parsley leaves, lemon wedges, chili flakes, and crusty bread as garnish.

Serving Suggestion: Use freshly torn Italian parsley leaves, lemon wedges, and chili flakes as garnish, and serve with crusty bread.

Variation Tip: Add spices of your choice.

Nutritional Information per Serving:

Calories 447kcal | Carbohydrates 30g | Sugars 7g | Sodium 0.30g | Fat 17g | Protein 41g | Fiber 5g

Salmon With Chia Seeds, Fennel Slaw, and Pickled Onions

Preparation Time: 20 minutes
Cooking Time: 10 minutes
Serves: 2

Ingredients:

For the pan-seared salmon:

- 2 x 4 to 6 oz. wild salmon (or steelhead trout) filets
- ½ tsp. salt
- ¼ tsp. pepper
- ½ tsp. dried mint, dill, or tarragon
- ½ tsp. granulated garlic
- 2 tsp. chia seeds
- 1 tbsp. olive oil
- ½ lemon (to finish)

For the fennel slaw:

- 1 extra-large fennel bulb, very thinly sliced (a mandolin is great for this)
- 1 Turkish cucumber
- ¼ cup thinly sliced sweet onion
- ½ oz. dill or tarragon
- 2 tbsp. olive oil
- 2 to 3 tbsp. lemon juice
- Salt and pepper to taste

Preparation:

1. Prepare the fennel slaw. In a medium-size mixing bowl, combine the slaw Ingredients and toss thoroughly, seasoning with salt and lemon if needed. Set aside.
2. Brush some of the olive oil over the top of the salmon filets.
3. Combine the salt, pepper, dried herbs, granulated garlic, and chia seeds in a small mixing bowl.
4. Apply the chia mixture liberally over the top of the fish, pushing it down with your fingers all the way to the edges.
5. Heat the remaining olive oil in a pan over medium heat. Let the pan get hot.
6. Pan-fry the fish for 3 to 4 minutes, chia seed side down, until brown and crispy. Turn the filets over gently with a metal spatula to keep the crust intact and continue cooking until the fish is cooked (3 to 4 minutes or more depending on thickness).
7. Place the fennel slaw on two plates and top with the fish.

Serving Suggestion: Top the fish with pickled red onions and fresh dill and a squeeze of lemon and serve it with bread or tortillas.

Variation Tip: Use spices to add flavor to the herb crust.

Nutritional Information per Serving:

Calories 399kcal | Carbohydrates 12g | Sugars 7g | Sodium 0.37g | Fat 27g | Protein 30g | Fiber 3g

Moroccan Salmon

Preparation Time: 5 minutes
Cooking Time: 12 minutes
Serves: 2

Ingredients:

- 2 (thick) salmon filets, 4 to 6 oz. each
- ½ tsp. cinnamon
- ½ tsp. cumin
- ½ tsp. salt
- ¾ tsp. sugar (or brown sugar)
- pinch cayenne or smoked paprika
- 1 tbsp. oil for searing

Preparation:

1. Preheat the oven to 350°F.

2. Combine the cinnamon, cumin, salt, sugar, and cayenne in a small bowl.

3. Season both sides of the salmon with the mixture.

4. In an oven-safe skillet (cast iron), heat the oil over medium-high heat. Sear the salmon filets o
both sides for 2 minutes, then finish in the oven for 5 minutes or until desired doneness is achieved.

Serving Suggestion: Garnish with orange zest and serve with bread or tortillas.

Variation Tip: Add spices of your choice to the mixture.

Nutritional Information per Serving:
Calories 297kcal | Protein 38g | Carbohydrates 3g | Fiber 1g | Sugars 2mg | Fat 15g | Sodium 0.71g

Brazilian Fish Stew

Preparation Time: 20 minutes
Cooking Time: 20 minutes
Serves: 4

Ingredients:

For the fish:

1 to 1½ lb. firm white fish—halibut, black cod, sea bass (thicker cuts are best)
½ tsp. salt
1 lime—zest and juice

For the stew/sauce:

2 to 3 tbsp. coconut or olive oil (or use Dende oil for the best flavor!)
1 onion, finely diced (red, white, or yellow)
½ tsp. salt
1 cup carrot, diced
1 red bell pepper, diced
4 garlic cloves, roughly chopped
½ jalapeno, finely diced
1 tbsp. tomato paste
2 tsp. paprika
1 tsp. ground cumin (or whole seed)
1 cup fish or chicken stock
1½cups tomatoes, diced (preferably fresh)
1 can (14 oz.) coconut milk (liquid and solids)
More salt to taste
½ cup chopped cilantro, scallions, or Italian parsley
Squeeze of lime

Preparation:

1. Cut the fish into 2-inch pieces after rinsing and patting them dry.
2. Place in a mixing bowl with 1 tablespoon of lime juice, salt, and half a lime's zest. Lightly massage to coat all pieces evenly. Set aside.
3. Heat the olive oil in a large sauté pan over medium-high heat. Sauté the onion and salt for 2 to 3 minutes. Reduce the heat to medium and add the carrots, bell pepper, garlic, and jalapeño and simmer for another 4 to 5 minutes.
4. Combine the tomato paste, spices, and stock in a large mixing bowl. Toss everything together and put in the sauté pan. Simmer on low before adding the tomatoes.
5. Cover the pan and cook for 5 minutes on medium-low, or until the carrots are soft.
6. Add the coconut milk and taste and season with additional salt if necessary.
7. Place the fish in the stew and heat it gently for 4 to 6 minutes, or until it is cooked through. You can also finish the stew off in a 350°F oven.
8. Season to taste with salt and lime juice.
9. If desired, drizzle with a little olive oil.

Serving Suggestion: Serve over rice with a squeeze of lime and a sprinkling of cilantro or scallions.

Variation Tip: Add more spices for a deeper flavor.

Nutritional Information per Serving:

Calories 404kcal | Carbohydrates 12g | Sugars 5g | Sodium 0.50g | Fat 20g | Protein 44g | Fiber 3g

Baja Taco Bowls

Preparation Time: 10 minutes
Cooking Time: 10 minutes
Serves: 4

Ingredients:

For the Baja battered fish:

- 1 lb. wild cod (or raw peeled shrimp, or cubed tofu)
- ½ cup all-purpose flour, spooned and leveled (or gluten-free flour blend)
- ½ tsp. salt
- ½ granulated garlic powder
- ½ tsp. chili powder
- ½ tsp. cumin
- ½ tsp. smoked paprika
- ½ tsp. oregano
- ½ cup beer
- ¼ cup oil for frying (high heat oil)

For the Baja bowl (pick a few out, you don't need to use them all!):

- Cilantro lime rice
- Mexican pinto beans
- Canned seasoned black beans
- Mexican slaw
- Chipotle mayo or creamy avocado sauce
- Pickled red onions
- Fresh veggies: sliced radishes, cucumber, cilantro, green onions, grated carrots, sprouts, or avocado. Limes!
- Crumbled queso fresco cheese (optional)
- Hot sauce

Preparation:

1. Prepare any of the Baja bowl Ingredients that you like. (It's better if you do this ahead of time.)
2. Cut the fish into four pieces. Allow them to air dry.
3. To make the batter: In a medium bowl, pour ½ cup beer. Combine all of the spices and salt in a mixing bowl. Whisk in the flour gradually. Add a bit of extra beer if you want a looser or thinner batter. Place the fish in the batter and turn it over to cover all sides.
4. To fry the fish: In a pan over medium heat, heat the oil until it is smoking hot (350°F) or sizzles when a drop of batter is dropped in. Place the battered fish in the oil with care, being careful not to let it spatter. Cook for 3 minutes or until the fish releases spontaneously from the pan (it will release when crispy and brown), then carefully flip it. Reduce the heat to low. Cook until the side is brown and crispy and the fish is cooked through. While you plate the bowls, place the fish on a paper towel-lined plate to absorb any excess oil. (If you want them to stay crispy, put them on a wire rack in a 300°F oven until ready to serve.)
5. Make the bowls' foundation with heated beans, rice, or both, then top with vegetables, avocado, and/or slaw. Serve with the fish on top. Serve with lime wedges and chipotle mayonnaise or spicy sauce on the side.

Serving Suggestion: Feel free to serve in tacos instead, cutting the fish into 1-inch-thick strips.

Variation Tip: You can use raw peeled shrimp or cubed tofu instead of the fish.

Nutritional Information per Serving:
Calories 249kcal | Carbohydrates 15g | Sugars 2.1g | Sodium 0.42g | Fat 11g | Protein 22g | Fiber 1g

Pan-Seared Steelhead Trout

Preparation Time: 30 minutes
Cooking Time: 30 minutes
Serves: 4

Ingredients:

   4 x 4 oz. pieces steelhead trout, salmon, halibut, sea bass (or try scallops!)
   3 cups baby new potatoes
   1 shallot, diced (or ¼ cup red onion)
   8 oz. mushrooms (cremini, shiitake, or morels)
   1 tbsp. olive oil
   1 tbsp. butter
   Salt and pepper to taste

For the spring pea truffle sauce:

   2 cups freshly shucked peas, blanched briefly (or use frozen)
   ½ cup water plus 1 tbsp. more, if necessary, to get the blender going.
   2 tbsp. olive oil
   1 tbsp. fresh lemon juice
   1 tbsp. truffle oil
   ¾ tsp. salt
   ¼ tsp. white pepper
   1 small garlic clove
   ⅓ cup fresh tarragon, basil, mint, or Italian parsley.

Preparation:

1. Cook the baby potatoes in salted boiling water, about 15 to 20 minutes.
2. The fresh peas should be blanched in salted boiling water for 2 minutes or until they float. To halt the heating process, shock them with ice-cold water (to help them stay green).
3. Blend the peas with the rest of the pea sauce Ingredients in a blender until creamy. In a saucepan, combine the Ingredients.
4. Over medium heat, sauté the mushrooms and shallots in butter until soft, about 5 to 7 minutes. Set aside after seasoning with salt and pepper.
5. Season the fish on both sides with salt and pepper.
6. Heat the oil in a large skillet over medium-high heat. Sear the fish, skin side down, until brown and crispy, about 3 to 4 minutes once the pan is heated. Cook the fish for a few minutes more on the other side, or place it in a heated oven.
7. Drain the potatoes and keep them aside. Heat the pea sauce gradually over medium heat, without boiling, to keep the color bright.
8. To serve, divide the pea sauce amongst the dishes. The potatoes come first, followed by the fish. Serve skin side up to preserve the skin's crispiness. Add the mushrooms on top. Finish with a sprig of fresh herb and a few drops of truffle oil over the mushrooms. Serve immediately and enjoy!

Serving Suggestion: Serve with a tortilla.

Variation Tip: Add spices of your choice.

Nutritional Information per Serving:
Calories 404kcal | Carbohydrates 28g | Protein 29.8g | Fat: 22.5g | Sodium 1.15g | Fiber 6g | Sugar 5g

Grilled Salmon With Avocado and Cucumber Salsa

Preparation Time: 25 minutes
Cooking Time: 8 minutes
Serves:4

Ingredients:

For the Mexican spiced salmon:
- 4 x 6 oz. salmon filets
- 1 tsp. salt
- ½ tsp. pepper
- 2 tsp. cumin
- 2 tsp. chili powder
- Lime for garnish

For the avocado salsa:

- 1 avocado (ripe, but slightly firm), diced
- 1 cup cucumber, diced
- ½ jalapeno, finely chopped
- ¼ cup cilantro, chopped
- 1 lime's juice and zest
- 2 to 3 tsp. olive oil
- ½ tsp. salt

For the creamy yogurt dressing:

- ½ cup plain Greek yogurt
- Lime juice from one small lime
- 1 garlic clove, minced
- 1 tbsp. olive oil
- ⅛ cup cilantro, chopped

- ½ tsp. salt
- ½ tsp. pepper
- 3 to 4 heads Little Gem lettuce (or baby romaine) per person

Preparation:

1. Preheat the broiler to medium-high temperature.
2. Make the spice rub in a small bowl by combining the salt, pepper, chili powder, and cumin. Rub the spice rub all over the fish.
3. Toss the salsa together. In a medium mixing bowl, combine all the Ingredients except the avocado. Fold in the avocado last to keep it intact, and don't overmix; you don't want it to get mushy.
4. In a small mixing dish, combine all of the Ingredients for the yogurt salad dressing.
5. Quarter the lettuce vertically. Set aside.
6. Broil the salmon for a few minutes on each side over medium heat or until the desired doneness is achieved. Medium to medium-rare is preferable. Use a thin metal spatula to turn the fish. Squeeze in a pinch of lime juice.
7. To assemble the dish: Toss the lettuce with a little dressing, just enough to coat it, and place it on a plate to make a "bed" for the salmon. Place the salmon on top, followed by the avocado salsa. Serve with lime wedges and cilantro.

Serving Suggestion: Serve with bread or tortilla.

Variation Tip: You can also pan-sear the salmon in a little olive oil or use a broiler pan.

Nutritional Information per Serving:
Calories 519kcal | Carbohydrates 31.5g | Sugars 9.1g | Sodium 1.35g | Fat 26g | Protein 49g | Fiber 15g

Baked Haddock With Tomato and Fennel

Preparation Time: 10 minutes
Cooking Time: 40 minutes
Serves: 4

Ingredients:

1 lb. haddock (or other white fish like cod, halibut, sable, or bass)
1½ tbsp. olive oil
3 cloves garlic, minced
1 lemon, juice and zest
½ tsp. kosher salt
¼ tsp. cracked pepper
1 tbsp. thyme
½ sweet onion, thinly sliced
Pinch salt and pepper
1 tsp. olive oil
1 fennel bulb, very thinly sliced
1½ lb. cherry, grape, or baby heirloom tomatoes

Preparation:

1. Preheat the oven to 400°F.
2. Using a knife, cut the fish into 6 to 8 pieces.
3. Combine the oil, garlic, salt, pepper, thyme, and lemon zest in a medium mixing bowl. Toss the fish in the mixture and set it aside.
4. Place the onion slices in the bottom of a lightly greased baking dish. The fennel slices should be strewn across the top. Drizzle with 1 teaspoon of olive oil, 12 teaspoons of lemon juice, and a liberal pinch of salt and pepper. Toss with tomatoes.
5. Place the dish in the oven and bake for 30 to 35 minutes, shaking it halfway through.
6. Place the fish nestled in between the tomatoes. Any leftover marinade should be drizzled over the fish and tomatoes. Return to the oven and cook for another 7 to 8 minutes, or until the fish is cooked to your liking.
7. Remove the dish from the oven. Serve with the lemon slices, and thyme sprinkled on top.

Serving Suggestion: Serve with rice or bread.

Variation Tip: Add a sprinkling of spices on the top of the fish before baking.

Nutritional Information per Serving:
Calories 365kcal | Carbohydrates 27g | Fat 19g | Sodium 1.23g | Sugar 7g | Protein 40g | Fiber 7g

Slow-Cooked Lamb Shanks

Preparation Time: 15 minutes
Cooking Time: 3 hours
Serves: 4

Ingredients:

- 3 tbsp. olive oil
- 4 lamb shanks
- 2 celery stalks, chopped
- 1 large onion, chopped
- 2 large carrots, chopped
- 6 cloves large garlic, chopped
- 1 tsp. anchovy paste
- 2 tsp. ground cinnamon
- 2 large bay leaves
- 6 juniper berries
- 2 tbsp. tomato paste
- 1 cup vermouth or white wine
- 4 cups lamb stock (if you don't have access to lamb stock, use 2 cups chicken and 2 cups beef)
- 3 tbsp. all-purpose flour
- Salt and pepper to taste
- A good handful of fresh parsley, chopped

Preparation:

1. Preheat the slow cooker on low.
2. In a large saucepan, heat the oil over medium-high heat. Season the lamb with salt and pepper on all sides. Brown the lamb on both sides in the pot.
3. Place the meat in the slow cooker.
4. Sauté all the veggies in a pan for 3 to 5 minutes to soften somewhat. Sprinkle the flour over the veggies and toss to coat.
5. Combine the tomato and anchovy paste in a mixing bowl. Add the cinnamon, juniper berries, salt and pepper and mix well.
6. Combine the stock and vermouth in a saucepan. On medium heat, bring to a boil, stirring regularly to cook off the alcohol and thicken the sauce.
7. Pour the vegetable/sauce combination over the lamb in the slow cooker. Cook the lamb for 3 hours on high or 5 hours on medium or 8 hours on low.

Serving Suggestion: Serve with mashed potatoes.

Variation Tip: Add more spices of your choice.

Nutritional Information per Serving:
Calories 455kcal | Carbohydrates 17g | Fat 17g | Sodium 0.63g | Sugar 4g | Protein 45g | Fiber 2g

Beef Massaman Thai Curry

Preparation Time: 20 minutes
Cooking Time: 1 hour and 30 minutes.
Serves: 4

Ingredients:

For the Massaman paste:

1 large onion, chopped
5 cloves of garlic, chopped
2 lemongrass stalks, tender part only, finely chopped
1-inch piece fresh ginger, peeled and grated
1 tbsp. ground cumin
1 tbsp. ground cilantro
8 black peppercorns
1 tsp. anchovy paste
1 tsp. granulated sugar
2 tbsp. vegetable oil

For the main dish:

1 lb. small potatoes, peeled and quartered
12 pearl onions, peeled and left whole
2 lb. beef stewing meat, cubed
Small bunch fresh cilantro stalks, finely chopped and separated
2-inch piece fresh root ginger, finely grated
2 x 14 oz cans coconut milk
1 tbsp. lime juice
1 tbsp. lemon juice
1 tbsp. fish sauce
3 leaves dried kaffir lime

Preparation:

1. Preheat the oven to 300°F.
2. In a dry frying pan, sauté the onion, garlic, lemongrass, ginger, cumin, ground cilantro, cloves, and peppercorns until aromatic (4 to 5 minutes).
3. Turn off the heat and set the pan aside to cool.
4. In a food processor, combine the spices, then add the anchovy paste, sugar, and oil and process until smooth. Set the mixture (the Massaman paste) aside.
5. Brown the beef in a large non-stick frying pan till golden brown, then transfer to a large oven-safe dish with the potatoes and onions.
6. In a frying pan, combine the Massaman paste, cilantro stems, and ginger, and cook for a few minutes until aromatic.
7. Add the coconut milk and bring the mixture to a boil, stirring constantly.
8. Season with the lime and lemon juice and fish sauce, add the lime leaves, then pour the sauce over the meat, onion, and potatoes. Cover with a lid and bake for 1½ hours.

Serving Suggestion: Serve on rice sprinkled with chopped cilantro leaves.

Variation Tip: Add spices of your choice.

Nutritional Information per Serving:
Calories 205kcal | Carbohydrates 31g | Protein 5g | Fat 7g | Sodium 0.42g | Fiber 5g | Sugar 6g

Beef and Broccoli Stir-Fry

Preparation Time: 10 minutes
Cooking Time: 10 minutes.
Serves: 4

Ingredients:

- 1 lb. steak
- 1 lb. broccoli, cut into bite-sized pieces

For the marinade:

- 2 tbsp. Shaoxing rice wine or sherry
- 1 tbsp. light soy sauce
- 1 tsp. canola oil
- 1 tsp. cornstarch
- ½ tsp. baking soda
- black pepper

For the stir-fry sauce:

- 2 tbsp. oyster sauce
- 2 tbsp. light soy sauce
- 1 tbsp. dark soy sauce
- ¼ cup water

- 1 tbsp. cornstarch
- 1 tsp. brown sugar
- Freshly ground black pepper

For the stir-fry:

- 2 tbsp. canola oil
- 2 cloves garlic, minced
- 1 shallot, chopped

- 2 tsp. fresh ginger, grated
- 2 green onions, sliced

Preparation:

1. Combine 12 teaspoons of baking soda with a tablespoon of water in a small mixing dish.
2. Using a sharp knife, cut the meat into thin strips (cutting against the grain). Toss the meat in th
mixture to coat it.
3. In a large mixing bowl, combine all the marinade Ingredients Add the beef and leave to sit whil
you prepare the rest of the dish.
4. Steam the broccoli until it is barely tender. To stop the broccoli from cooking any further, place
in a bath of cold water for approximately a minute. Set aside after removing from the ice bath using
slotted spoon.
5. In a small mixing bowl, combine all the stir-fry sauce Ingredients and set aside.
6. Heat the oil over high heat in a skillet or wok, then add the meat and cook for 1 to 2 minute
(leaving some of it pink). Remove the meat from the pan and set it aside.
7. Add the garlic, shallot, and ginger to the pan and cook for another 30 seconds. Toss in the brocco
and mix well. Put the meat back in the pan, along with the stir-fry sauce and green onions. Allow th
sauce to thicken by mixing everything together.

Serving Suggestion: Serve with steamed rice.

Variation Tip: Replace the oyster sauce with hoisin sauce or teriyaki sauce for a simple variation.

Nutritional Information per Serving:
Calories 393kcal | Carbohydrates 15g | Protein 28g | Fat 25g | Sodium 1.48g | Fiber 3g | Sugar 4g

Beef Stroganoff

Preparation Time: 15 minutes
Cooking Time: 15 minutes.
Serves: 4

Ingredients:

2 tbsp. olive oil
2 tbsp. butter
1½ lb. beef sirloin steak, cut into ½ inch strips
1 large onion, chopped
2 garlic cloves, minced
1 lb. fresh mushrooms, sliced
2 tsp. dry mustard
3 tbsp. all-purpose flour
⅓ cup white wine or dry vermouth
2 cups beef stock
¼ cup sour cream
Salt and pepper
Fresh parsley, chopped

Preparation:

1. In a large pan, sear the meat strips on both sides quickly (steak overcooks quickly, so a minute or two is all you need). Remove with a slotted spoon from the pan, transfer to a dish, and set aside.
2. Add 2 tablespoons of butter to the pan and return it to the heat. When the butter has melted, add the onions and cook until they are transparent. Stir in the mushrooms until everything is well combined. Continue to sauté for another 5 to 7 minutes, or until the mushrooms are cooked and the onions are soft.
3. Add the garlic and cook for another minute. Mix in the flour and mustard powder until thoroughly combined. Cook for another minute or two to let the flour absorb the liquid.
4. To deglaze the pan, add the wine or vermouth and scrape the brown pieces from the bottom of the pan into the white wine. Allow for another 3 minutes of cooking time.
5. Stir in the beef stock until everything is well combined. Let the mixture simmer for 5 minutes, stirring occasionally.
6. Remove the pan from the heat and whisk in the sour cream until smooth, then add the cooked steak back to the pan. Season to taste, then season with salt and pepper if necessary.

Serving Suggestion: Serve with egg noodles, rice, or potatoes, and parsley on top if preferred.

Variation Tip: For extra flavor, marinate the steak strips in two tablespoons of soy sauce for 15 minutes before cooking.

Nutritional Information per Serving:
Calories 455kcal | Carbohydrates 14g | Protein 45g | Fat 23g | Sodium 0.40g | Fiber 3g | Sugar 5g

Italian Beef Stew

Preparation Time: 20 minutes
Cooking Time: 1 hour and 30 minutes.
Serves: 4

Ingredients:

- 2 lb. stewing beef, cubed
- 2 tbsp. flour
- 1 tbsp. olive oil
- 1 large onion, chopped
- 3 cloves garlic, chopped
- 1 cup white wine
- 3 tbsp. tomato paste
- 3 cups beef stock
- 14 oz. mushrooms, sliced (any variety)
- 3 large carrots, sliced
- 2 stalks of celery, sliced
- A good handful of fresh parsley, chopped
- Salt and pepper
- 1 lb. pasta of your choice

Preparation:

1. Preheat the oven to 350°F.
2. Season the meat with salt and pepper before dredging it in the flour.
3. In a large oven-safe saucepan, heat the oil over medium heat. Cook the meat until it is golde brown on both sides (I did this in two batches to avoid crowding the pan).
4. Remove the meat from the pan and set it aside.
5. In the same pan, sauté the onions until they are transparent (about 5 minutes).
6. Add the garlic and cook for another minute.
7. Raise the heat to medium-high and add the wine. Cook the wine until it has been reduced to ha its original volume.
8. Anything that has clung to the bottom of the pan may be scraped up and stirred in.
9. Add the tomato paste and mix well.
10. Toss the meat back into the pan.
11. Combine the veggies and stock in a mixing bowl. Season the veggies and stock with salt an pepper to taste and add to the pan.
12. Cover the pan and bake in the oven for 1½ hours.
13. Bring a big saucepan of water to a boil, then follow the package directions for cooking.

Serving Suggestion: Serve the stew on top of the pasta.

Variation Tip: Use cheese and more herbs and spices.

Nutritional Information per Serving:
Calories 698kcal | Carbohydrates 105g | Protein 23g | Fat 16g | Sodium 0.51g | Fiber 7g | Sugar 11

Slow-Cooked Italian Pulled Pork

Preparation Time: 15 minutes
Cooking Time: 8 hours
Serves: 6

Ingredients:

1 boneless pork shoulder roast
1 tsp. salt
Black pepper and salt, to taste
2 tbsp. olive oil, separated
6 cloves garlic, minced
1 onion, diced
28 oz. can crushed tomatoes
3 tbsp. tomato paste
1 cup red or white wine (whatever you prefer)
2 good handfuls fresh basil, torn
1 good handful fresh parsley, chopped

For the sandwich:

Italian bread
Mozzarella cheese

Preparation:

1. In a big saucepan, heat the olive oil, then add the onion and simmer for 4 to 5 minutes, or until softened.
2. Add the garlic and cook for another minute.
3. Dilute the tomato paste in a glass of the wine. Increase the heat to high, mix in the diluted tomato paste, and cook until the liquid has been reduced by one-third.
4. Place the meat in a slow cooker.
5. Add the tomatoes, basil, and parsley to the wine mixture after the diluted wine has decreased. Stir in a pinch of salt and black pepper.
6. Bring the sauce to a boil before spooning it over the meat in the slow cooker.
7. Cook for 8 hours on low.
8. Place the pork on a chopping board and tear it apart with two forks.
9. To put together the sandwich: Pile the pulled pork on top of the Italian bread. Cover with a thin layer of sauce followed by shredded mozzarella cheese. Broil until the cheese has melted.

Serving Suggestion: Serve with a dip of your choice.

Variation Tip: Use different spices.

Nutritional Information per Serving:
Calories 541kcal | Carbohydrates 5g | Protein 31g | Fat 36g | Sodium 0.56g | Fiber 5g | Sugar 7g

Beef Brisket Soup

Preparation Time: 20 minutes
Cooking Time: 8 hours
Serves: 5

Ingredients:

- 1 tbsp. olive oil
- 2 lb. beef brisket (not corned beef)
- Salt and freshly ground black pepper, to taste
- 1 large onion, chopped
- 4 carrots, sliced
- 3 stalks celery, diced
- 2 garlic cloves, minced
- A good handful of fresh parsley, chopped, including stems
- 2 bay leaves
- 6 cups beef stock
- 3 large potatoes, peeled and cubed
- ½ lb. pasta or noodles of your choice

Preparation:

1. Heat the olive oil in a large saucepan. Brown the brisket on both sides over medium-high heat, seasoning it with salt and pepper.
2. Remove the brisket and set it aside.
3. Cook the onions, carrots, celery, and garlic (stirring periodically) for 5 minutes over medium heat before they begin to brown in the fat in the saucepan.
4. Along with the bay leaves, add the potatoes and parsley to the saucepan.
5. Season the brisket with salt and pepper and return it to the saucepan with the liquid.
6. Raise the heat to high and bring the mixture to a boil. Transfer to a slow cooker, cover, and simmer for 8 to 10 hours on low heat.
7. Remove the brisket from the saucepan and slice or tear it apart using a fork to get shredded meat.
8. Remove the bay leaves and the fat using a skimmer.
9. Meanwhile, bring a pasta pot of water to a boil, then cook and drain the pasta according to package directions.
10. To serve, divide the pasta into bowls and top with the hot soup.

Serving Suggestion: Serve with a sprinkling of herbs of your choice.

Variation Tip: You can add vegetables of your choice to the slow cooker.

Nutritional Information per Serving:
Calories 620kcal | Carbohydrates 61g | Protein 54g | Fat 17g | Sodium 0.78g | Fiber 6g | Sugar 6g

Meatloaf

Preparation Time: 15 minutes
Cooking Time: 55 minutes.
Serves: 10

Ingredients:

5 oz. breadcrumbs (about 2 cups)
½ cup milk or water (plus more if needed)
2 tbsp. olive oil or butter
1 large onion, chopped
½ tsp. baking soda
1 tbsp. water
2 lb. ground beef (80%–85% lean)
2 large eggs
3 tbsp. ketchup
1 tsp. salt
2 tsp. Bell's Seasoning (optional)
2 tbsp. fresh parsley, chopped
Freshly grated black pepper to taste

For the glaze:

¼ cup ketchup
1 tbsp. brown sugar
1 tbsp. low-sodium soy sauce

Preparation:

1. Preheat the oven to 350°F.
2. Combine the breadcrumbs and milk in a small mixing bowl and whisk until thoroughly moistened. Leave them to soak while you're sautéing the onion.
3. In a skillet, sauté the onions in oil or butter until they are tender. Allow them to cool before serving.
4. Combine 12 teaspoons of baking soda with a tablespoon of water in a small mixing dish.
5. Pour the baking soda mixture over the beef in a large mixing bowl, then add the eggs, cooled onions, parsley, ketchup, Bell's Seasoning, parsley, salt, and pepper. Mix everything together with your hands until completely mixed (but not over-mixed!).
6. Place the meat mixture in a roasting pan coated with non-stick foil (or parchment paper). Form it into a loaf form by pushing it together with your hands.
7. Combine all of the glaze Ingredients in a smaller bowl. Distribute equally across the top of the meatloaf.
8. Bake the meatloaf for 55 minutes (or until its internal temperature reaches 160°F).
9. Allow it to rest for 10 minutes before serving (lightly tented with foil to keep it warm).

Serving Suggestion: Serve with a fresh salad.

Variation Tip: Use other seasonings or sauce of your choice.

Nutritional Information per Serving:
Calories 282kcal | Carbohydrates 16g | Protein 21g | Fat 13g | Sodium 0.61g | Fiber 7g | Sugar 5g

Oven-Baked Meatballs

Preparation Time: 20 minutes
Cooking Time: 20 minutes.
Serves: 4

Ingredients:

- 5 oz. breadcrumbs (about 2 cups)
- ½ cup milk or water (plus more if needed)
- ½ tsp. baking soda
- 1 tbsp. water
- 2 lb. ground beef (80%–85% lean)
- 2 large eggs
- 6 garlic cloves, minced
- A good handful fresh parsley, chopped
- 1 cup parmesan cheese, freshly grated
- Salt to taste (I use at least a tbsp. of salt)
- Freshly ground black pepper (about 15 turns of the grinder)

Preparation:

1. Before you start making the meatballs, preheat the oven to 400°F. Coat two non-stick baking pan well with some non-stick cooking spray.
2. Combine the baking soda and water in a small mixing bowl, then pour the mixture over th breadcrumbs and stir thoroughly.
3. Add the milk and whisk to combine while adding additional milk if necessary. To completely wet th breadcrumbs, add 1 tablespoon at a time. Allow the mixture to rest while you prepare the remainin Ingredients.
4. Season the meat, garlic, parsley, and parmesan cheese with approximately a teaspoon of salt an freshly grated pepper in a large bowl. Mix in the breadcrumb mixture with your hands. Press th mixture between your fingers until it is completely mixed. Form the Ingredients into even-size meatballs using oiled hands.
5. Place the formed meatballs on the baking pans, spreading them equally apart (approximately 2 per pan). Bake the meatballs in the oven for 20 minutes, turning halfway through. Cook until they ar cooked through, and an internal meat thermometer reads 160°F.

Serving Suggestion: Serve with pasta of your choosing.

Variation Tip: Use more of your favorite spices or seasoning.

Nutritional Information per Serving:
Calories 197kcal | Carbohydrates 8g | Protein 22g | Fat 9g | Sodium 0g | Fiber 5g | Sugar 2g

Braised Pork in Sweet Soy Sauce

Preparation Time: 10 minutes
Cooking Time: 30 minutes
Serves: 4

Ingredients:

2 lb. pork loin
2 tbsp. vegetable oil
1 tbsp. garlic and ginger paste
1 tbsp. olive oil
1 tbsp. sesame oil
½ cup soy sauce
4 tbsp. sugar
1½ cup water
1 tbsp. chili garlic sauce

Garnish (optional):

2 green onions, chopped

Preparation:

1. Cut the pork into 1-inch pieces. Sauté for 3 minutes over medium-high heat in a skillet with the vegetable oil until the meat is no longer pink and is starting to brown.

2. Combine the remaining Ingredients in a medium mixing bowl and then pour over the meat. Bring the liquid to a boil. There may appear to be too much water, but it will be reduced.

3. Once the liquid is boiling, reduce the heat to low and allow it to simmer for around 30 minutes, stirring occasionally, or until there are only about 3 tablespoons of sauce left.

4. Garnish with the green onions

Serving Suggestion: Serve over noodles or steamed rice.

Variation Tip: Use more herbs and spices of your choice.

Nutritional Information per Serving:
Calories 495kcal | Carbohydrates 16g | Protein 53g | Fat 23g | Sodium 1.38g | Fiber 1g | Sugar 13g

Spicy Vegetable Stew With Coconut

Preparation Time: 10 minutes
Cooking Time: 40 minutes.
Serves: 4

Ingredients:

- 1 tbsp. rapeseed oil
- 2 large onions, thinly sliced
- 1 tbsp. finely chopped ginger
- 3 garlic cloves, chopped
- 1 large red chili, deseeded and thinly sliced
- 1 tbsp. thyme leaves
- 1 tsp. cinnamon
- 1 tsp. smoked paprika
- 2 tsp. ground cilantro
- 2 tsp. cumin seeds
- 2 x 14 oz. cans chopped tomatoes
- 3$\frac{1}{3}$ cups vegetable bouillon made with 4 tsp. vegetable bouillon powder
- 2 green peppers, seeded and cubed
- 1 sweet potato, seeded and cubed
- 2 plantains, peeled and sliced
- 5.6 oz. brown basmati rice
- 2 x 14 oz. cans red kidney beans, drained
- Handful fresh cilantro, chopped (plus extra for sprinkling)
- 4 tbsp. unsweetened coconut yogurt

Preparation:

1. Heat the oil in a large non-stick skillet and cook the onions for 8 minutes, or until they are softened and golden.
2. Add the ginger, garlic, chili, and thyme and cook for another minute, stirring occasionally. Stir in the spices for a few seconds over high heat, then add the tomatoes and bouillon, followed by the peppers, sweet potato, and plantains. Cover the mixture with a lid and cook for 30 minutes on low heat.
3. Meanwhile, follow the package directions for boiling the rice. Stir the beans and cilantro into the stew and simmer for 10 minutes, or until the peppers are cooked.
4. To serve, divide half of the rice and stew between two dishes, top each with 2 tablespoons of yogurt and sprinkle with more cilantro.
5. Cool the leftover stew and rice, then cover and refrigerate until ready to serve again. To reheat the stew, do so gently in a pan with a splash of water until it starts to bubble. The rice can be reheated in the microwave.

Serving Suggestion: Serve with rice.

Variation Tip: Use fresh sliced tomatoes instead of canned.

Nutritional Information per Serving:
Calories 603kcal | Carbohydrates 97g | Protein 19g | Fat 11g | Sodium 0.3g | Fiber 21g | Sugar 28 g

Mushroom Buckwheat Risotto

Preparation Time: 15 minutes
Cooking Time: 30 minutes.
Serves: 4

Ingredients:

3 tbsp. butter
1 banana shallot, finely chopped
2 big garlic cloves, finely chopped
1 bay leaf
1½ cups buckwheat
²/₃ cup white wine
½ oz. dried porcini mushrooms soaked in 3¹/₃ cups water, drained, liquid reserved, and mushrooms chopped
7 oz. portobello mushrooms, sliced
9 oz. chestnut mushrooms, sliced

For the buraczki:

7 oz. cooked beetroot, grated
½ cup crème fraîche
1 tbsp. creamed horseradish
½ small pack dill, leaves chopped, plus some fronds to serve
Juice of ½ lemon

Preparation:

1. In a mixing bowl, combine all of the buraczki Ingredients, seasoning to taste, and set aside.
2. In a sauté pan over medium heat, melt 1 tablespoon of the butter. Add the shallot and a pinch of salt and cook, stirring periodically, for 8 minutes, or until softened but not browned.
3. Cook for 1 minute more after adding the garlic and bay leaf, then add the buckwheat. After 1 minute of toasting, pour in the wine. Add part of the mushroom liquid when the wine has nearly diminished and stir until it is absorbed.
4. Continue to add the liquid in small increments, stirring periodically, until all of the liquid has been used and the buckwheat is soft but somewhat chewy. This will take around 20 minutes.
5. Meanwhile, in a frying pan over high heat, melt the remaining butter. Fry the mushrooms for 5 minutes, or until all the liquid has evaporated and the mushrooms are golden. Don't worry if the butter turns brown; it will give a nice nutty flavor.
6. Add the mushrooms to the risotto, mix well, and season with salt and pepper to taste.

Serving Suggestion: Serve in dishes with the buraczki and dill fronds on top.

Variation Tip: Sprinkle the dish with cilantro.

Nutritional Information per Serving:
Calories 557kcal | Carbohydrates 71 g | Protein 11g | Fat 21g | Sodium 0.5g | Fiber 5g | Sugar 8g

Balsamic Lentil Pies With Vegetable Mash

Preparation Time: 15 minutes
Cooking Time: 45 minutes.
Serves: 4

Ingredients:

- 2 tbsp. rapeseed oil, plus a drop extra
- 4 red onions, thinly sliced
- 7 oz. puy lentils
- 2 tbsp. finely chopped rosemary
- 1 tbsp. vegetable bouillon powder
- 2 tbsp. balsamic vinegar
- 12 oz. celeriac, peeled and diced
- 12 oz. swede, peeled and diced
- 12 oz. potato, peeled and diced
- 11 oz. broccoli florets, divided
- 11 oz. spinach, spinach
- 2¼ oz. vegetarian Italian-style hard cheese, finely grated

Preparation:

1. In a large non-stick skillet, heat the oil and cook the onions for 8 minutes, or until softened and golden.
2. Bring a full pot of water (around 4 cups) to a boil. Stir in the lentils, rosemary, bouillon, and balsamic vinegar with the onions, then cover and cook for 35 to 40 minutes, or until the lentils are cooked but still have a bite.
3. Meanwhile, fully cook the root vegetables and half of the broccoli.
4. In a heated skillet with a touch of oil, wilt half of the spinach for 2 minutes.
5. Using a hand blender or masher, mash the root vegetables.
6. Place the lentils mixture in four separate pie plates, cover with the mash, and then sprinkle with the cheese.
7. Place the pie plates under the broiler to melt the cheese. Serve with the prepared green vegetables while they're still hot. Keep the remainder in the fridge until you're ready to use it (it will last for days). To reheat the pies, bake in the oven at 350°F for 35 mins.

Serving Suggestion: Cook the rest of the green veg (as above) to serve alongside.

Variation Tip: Add spices of your choice.

Nutritional Information per Serving:
Calories 457kcal | Carbohydrates 53g | Protein 26g | Fat 12g | Sodium 0.6g | Fiber 17g | Sugar 12g

Sweet Potato Parcel

Preparation Time: 15 minutes
Cooking Time: 1 hour and 15 minutes
Serves: 4

Ingredients:

- 4 sweet potatoes (1 lb. 10 oz.), peeled and cut into 1-inch chunks
- 5 tbsp. cold-pressed rapeseed oil
- 1 onion, thinly sliced
- 2 large garlic cloves, crushed
- ½ tsp. chili flakes
- 1 small bunch sage, leaves sliced
- 6½ oz. pack chestnuts, roughly chopped
- 3 tbsp. cranberry sauce
- 5 sheets filo pastry

Preparation:

1. Preheat the oven to 400°F. Place the potatoes chunks on a baking dish, drizzle with 1 tablespoon of the oil, season, and bake for 25 minutes.
2. While the potatoes are roasting, heat 1 tablespoon of the oil in a frying pan and soften the onion for 7 to 10 minutes over medium heat. Add the garlic and chili flakes and cook for another minute.
3. Remove from the heat and stir in the sweet potato cubes, chestnuts, and cranberry sauce. Season the mixture with salt and pepper.
4. Line an 8-inch square baking tin with a rectangle of baking paper that extends up to two edges. (This is to help you remove it later.) Brush the bottom and sides of the tin with a bit of the leftover oil, then add another sheet of filo going in the other way. Brush the bottom and sides of the filo with additional oil, then repeat with the remaining two sheets of filo.
5. Fill the tin with the sweet potato mixture and fold the filo over to top it, sprinkling with a little extra oil. Scrunch the last piece of filo on top of the package after brushing it with the leftover oil. Bake the parcel for 30 minutes in the oven.
6. To serve, take the package out of the tin using the baking parchment.

Serving Suggestion: Serve with a fresh salad.

Variation Tip: Add some more seasoning of your choice.

Nutritional Information per Serving:

Calories 567kcal | Fat 17g | Sodium 0.7g | Carbohydrates 90g | Fiber 9g | Sugar 27g | Protein 9g

Chickpea Fajitas

Preparation Time: 15 minutes
Cooking Time: 25 minutes
Serving: 2

Ingredients:

- 14 oz. can chickpeas
- 1 tbsp. olive oil
- Pinch of smoked paprika
- 2 tomatoes, deseeded and diced
- 1 small red onion, finely sliced
- 2 tbsp. red wine vinegar
- 1 avocado, stoned and peeled
- 2 limes, juice of 1, the other cut into wedges
- 3½oz. soured cream
- 2 tsp. harissa
- 4 corn tortillas

Preparation:

1. Preheat the oven to 400°F and line a baking tray with foil.
2. Drain the chickpeas, pat them dry, and place them on the baking tray. Toss in the oil and paprika to coat, then roast for 20 to 25 minutes, tossing halfway through, until golden and crisp.
3. Meanwhile, combine the tomatoes and onion with the vinegar in a small bowl and leave aside to pickle.
4. Put the avocado in a separate bowl and mash it with a fork, seasoning with salt and pepper after adding the lime juice.
5. Combine the soured cream and harissa in a mixing bowl and leave aside until ready to serve.
6. Heat a griddle pan until it is practically blazing hot. One at a time, add the tortillas and sear each side with griddle lines and until heated through.
7. Arrange the Ingredients on the table and assemble the fajitas: pour a little harissa cream over the tortilla, then top with the roasted chickpeas, guacamole, pickled salsa, and cilantro, if desired.

Serving Suggestion: Serve with lime wedges on the side.

Variation Tip: Use other spices of your choice.

Nutritional Information per Serving:
Calories 782kcal | Fat 36g | Sodium 1.5g | Carbohydrates 87g | Fiber 16g | Sugar 13g | Protein 17g

Spinach, Sweet Potato, and Lentil Dhal

Preparation Time: 10 minutes
Cooking Time: 35 minutes
Serves: 4

Ingredients:

1 tbsp. sesame oil
1 red onion, finely chopped
1 garlic clove, crushed
Thumb-sized piece ginger, peeled and finely chopped
1 red chili, finely chopped
1½ tsp. ground turmeric
1½ tsp. ground cumin
2 sweet potatoes (about 14oz), cut into even chunks
9 oz. red split lentils
2½ cups vegetable stock
3 oz. spinach
4 scallions, sliced on the diagonal, to serve
½ small pack of Thai basil, leaves torn, to serve

Preparation:

1. Heat the sesame oil in a wide-based pan with a tight-fitting cover.
2. Add the finely chopped red onion and cook for 10 minutes over medium heat, turning regularly, until softened
3. Add the garlic, ginger, red chili, turmeric, and cumin and cook for another minute.
4. Increase the heat to medium-high, then add the sweet potato pieces. Toss to coat the potatoes in the spice mixture.
5. Place the red split lentils, vegetable stock, and a pinch of salt and pepper in a large saucepan and place over a medium-high heat.
6. Bring the liquid to a boil. Lower the heat to low, cover, and simmer for 20 minutes. The lentils should be cooked, and the potato is barely maintaining its form.
7. Season to taste with salt and pepper, then gently fold in the spinach. To serve, top with the scallions and Thai basil leaves.

Serving Suggestion: Serve with brown rice.

Variation Tip: Add some extra spices.

Nutritional Information per Serving:
Calories 397kcal | Fat 5g | Sodium 0.7g | Carbohydrates 66g | Fiber 11g | Sugar 19g | Protein 18g

Butternut Chili

Preparation Time: 30 minutes
Cooking Time: 1 hour
Serves: 4

Ingredients:

- 1 lb. 5 oz. medium vine tomatoes or 14 oz can chopped or cherry tomatoes
- 2 tbsp. olive oil
- 2 onions, finely chopped
- 2 large garlic cloves, finely chopped
- 1 red bird's eye chili, deseeded and finely chopped
- 1 tsp. cayenne pepper
- 1 tsp. oregano
- 1 bay leaf
- 1 lb. 5 oz. butternut squash, peeled and cut into cubes
- 12 pitted green olives, roughly chopped
- $2/3$ cup red wine
- ½ vegetable stock cube
- 7 oz. jar piquillo pimiento peppers, or 2 roasted Romano peppers, roughly chopped
- 14 oz. can black beans or red kidney beans, drained and rinsed
- Small bunch chives, snipped
- ¾ cup soured cream

Preparation:

1. If using fresh tomatoes, pour boiling water over them in a bowl, count to 30, then lift them out peel and chop.
2. In a heavy-bottomed frying pan, heat the oil and add the onions and garlic. Gently soften, stirring once in a while. Toss the onions with the chili, cayenne, oregano, and bay leaf.
3. Stir in the squash, olives, and wine after 1 minute of stirring. Simmer for a few minutes, stirring occasionally, before adding the tomatoes and just under 1 cup of water. Stir in the stock cube after crumbling it. Bring to a low boil, then reduce to a low heat and cook for 30 minutes, stirring regularly.
4. Season with salt and pepper after adding the peppers to the pan. If it appears to be dry, add more water. Cook the mixture for another 25 to 30 minutes, or until the squash is soft. This step can be stored for up to 1 month; thaw overnight in the refrigerator before continuing with the procedure.
5. Add the beans to the pan and reheat.

Serving Suggestion: Serve with rice and sour cream on the side.

Variation Tip: Add more spices of your choice.

Nutritional Information per Serving:
Calories 370kcal | Fat 16g | Sodium 1.7g | Carbohydrates 33g | Fiber 11g | Sugar 16g | Protein 10g

Miso Eggplant

Preparation Time: 5 minutes
Cooking Time: 50 minutes
Serves: 2

Ingredients:

2 small eggplants, halved
Vegetable oil, for roasting and frying
2¼ oz. brown miso
3½ oz. giant couscous
1 red chili, thinly sliced
½ small pack cilantro, leaves chopped

Preparation:

1. Preheat the oven to 350°F. Criss-cross the flesh of the eggplants in a diagonal pattern using a sharp knife, then lay on a baking pan. Brush 1 tablespoon of the oil on the flesh.

2. To produce a thick paste, combine the miso and 1½ tablespoons of water. Spread the paste over the eggplants, then cover with foil and roast for 30 minutes in the center of the oven.

3. Remove the cover and continue to roast the eggplants for another 15 to 20 minutes, or until cooked, depending on their size.

4. Meanwhile, bring a pot of salted water to a boil and heat 12 tablespoons of vegetable oil in a frying pan over medium-high heat. In a frying pan, toast the couscous for 2 minutes until golden brown, then drop into a pan of boiling water and simmer for 8 to 10 minutes until cooked (or according to the package directions). Drain well.

Serving Suggestion: Serve the eggplants with the couscous, topped with the chili and a scattering of cilantro leaves.

Variation Tip: Add vegetarian sauce if you want.

Nutritional Information per Serving:
Calories 390kcal | Fat 12g | Sodium 2.7g | Carbohydrates 51g | Fiber 11g | Protein 18g | Sugars 8g

Smoky Tofu Tortillas

Preparation Time: 10 minutes
Cooking Time: 15 minutes
Servings: 4

Ingredients:

- 1 tbsp. vegetable or olive oil
- 2 onions, each cut into 12 wedges
- 2 Romano peppers, deseeded and sliced
- Small pack cilantro, leaves picked, stems finely chopped
- 2 tsp. ground cumin
- 1 tsp. hot smoked paprika
- 7 oz. pack smoked tofu (I like Taifun), cut into bite-sized pieces
- 14 oz. can kidney beans, drained and rinsed
- 14 oz. can cherry tomatoes
- 1 tbsp. dark brown soft sugar

To serve with:

- 8 corn and wheat tortillas
- 2 limes, cut into wedges
- Extra virgin olive oil, for drizzling
- 1 large ripe avocado, stoned, peeled, and sliced just before serving
- Thick yogurt or sour cream

Preparation:

1. In a large frying pan, heat the oil and add the onions and peppers. Season and cook for 8 minutes over high heat, or until barely tender and beginning to sear.
2. Add the cilantro stems and sauté for 1 minute (stirring constantly) before adding the spices and cooking for another 2 minutes until aromatic.
3. Cook for 5 minutes, or until the sauce is very dry. Add the tofu, beans, tomatoes, and sugar until the tofu is fully cooked. Warm the tortillas following pack instructions.
4. Season the sauce with salt and pepper, then stir in the cilantro leaves and a squeeze of lime.

Serving Suggestion: Serve with tortillas, lime halves, avocado, and yogurt or sour cream on the side, drizzled with extra virgin olive oil.

Variation Tip: You can add other spices to the sauce if you prefer.

Nutritional Information per Serving:
Calories 567kcal | Fat 16g | Sodium 1.3g | Carbohydrates 78g | Fiber 15g | Sugar 20g | Protein 19g

Nettle Gnudi With Wild Pesto

Preparation Time: 25 minutes
Cooking Time: 15 minutes
Servings: 4

Ingredients:

2 x 9 oz. tubs good-quality ricotta
7 oz. young nettle leaves
2 oz. parmesan (or vegetarian alternative), grated, plus extra to serve
2 egg yolks
Nutmeg, for grating
12 oz. semolina flour or fine semolina
6 tbsp. wild pesto

Preparation:

. Set a sieve over a bowl and line it with muslin. Place the ricotta on top, gather the muslin ends, and knot them together carefully. Drain the cheese for 4 hours, or better yet, overnight.

. In the meantime, bring a pot of water to a boil. Blanch the nettle leaves briefly in the boiling water, then drain and cool under cold running water. Drain well again, squeezing out as much water as possible from the leaves, then very finely chop and chill until needed.

. To create the gnudi, strain the ricotta into a large mixing bowl. Stir in all but a few tablespoons of the parmesan, the egg yolks, nettles, a good grating of nutmeg, and lots of salt and pepper. To mix, give it a thorough stir.

. Fill a large baking pan halfway with the semolina (it will need to fit in your fridge later). Wet your hands, dip them in semolina, then rapidly scoop 1 heaping teaspoon of the ricotta mixture onto your hands, rolling it into a ball. Place the ball on the semolina tray and roll it around to cover it fully. Pick it up and roll it between your palms to make a smooth ball, then return it to the semolina.

. Make sure the balls are properly spaced in the semolina before covering loosely with cling film. Chill for 12 to 24 hours—the longer, the better – until the gnudi has developed a skin.

. Bring a big pot of water to a boil for cooking the gnudi. In the meantime, put the pesto in a frying pan. Once the water is boiling, add the gnudi in batches. Cook them for 2 to 3 minutes, or until they float to the top. Using a slotted spoon, scoop out the contents and place them in a strainer. Repeat with the rest of the gnudi.

. To loosen the pesto, heat it in the pan with a few tablespoons of the gnudis' cooking water. Place the cooked gnudi in the frying pan with the pesto and gently flip the balls.

Serving Suggestion: Top with the remaining parmesan and a generous pinch of black pepper.

Variation Tip: Top the dish with another cheese of your choice.

Nutritional Information per Serving:
Calories 688kcal | Fat 33g | Sodium 0.7g | Carbohydrates 67g | Fiber 3g | Sugar 3g | Protein 29g

Green Salad

Preparation Time: 15 minutes
Cooking Time: 15 minutes
Servings: 8

Ingredients:

- ½ cup onion, chopped
- ½ cup green bell pepper, chopped
- 2 x 10 oz. packages mixed salad greens
- 4 thin slices chicken deli meat, chopped
- 1 tomato, chopped
- ¼ tsp. onion powder
- 3 dashes garlic powder
- 1 pinch ground black pepper
- 2 pinches salt
- 3 tbsp. balsamic vinaigrette salad dressing

Preparation:

1. Microwave or sauté the onion and bell pepper until soft; set aside to cool.
2. Combine the onion, pepper, salad greens, deli meat, and tomato in a large salad bowl. Sprinkle wit
the onion powder, garlic powder, black pepper, and salt. Toss to mix.
3. Pour on enough salad dressing or vinegar to coat, toss again and serve.

Serving Suggestion: Serve with any main dish.

Variation Tip: Add lemon.

Nutritional Information per Serving:
Calories 47kcal | Sodium 0.16g | Protein 2.6g | Carbohydrates 5.1g | Sugars 15.6g | Fat 2.3g | Fibe
2g

French Herb Salad

Preparation Time: 30 minutes
Cooking Time: 30 minutes
Serves: 8

Ingredients:

- 1 head romaine lettuce, rinsed, dried, and chopped
- 1 head red leaf lettuce, rinsed, dried, and chopped (optional)
- 1 leaf green leaf lettuce, rinsed, dried, and chopped (optional)
- 1 (5 oz.) package baby arugula leaves, washed and dried
- 1 head endive, rinsed, dried, and chopped
- 1 cup frisée lettuce leaves, rinsed, dried, and chopped
- 1 cup dandelion leaves, rinsed, dried, and chopped (optional)
- 1 cup escarole, rinsed, dried, and chopped (optional)
- 1 cup Batavia lettuce, rinsed, dried, and chopped (optional)
- 3 leaves fresh basil, chopped
- 3 leaves fresh tarragon, chopped
- 3 sprigs fresh dill, chopped

Preparation:

1. In a large salad bowl, add the romaine, red and green leaf lettuce, arugula, endive, frisée lettuce, dandelion leaves, escarole, Batavia lettuce, basil, tarragon, and dill.

Serving Suggestion: Serve with any main dish.

Variation Tip: Add more vegetables if you want.

Nutritional Information per Serving:

Calories 34kcal | Fat 0.5g | Sodium 0.04g | Carbohydrates 6.5g | Fiber 4.2g | Sugar 1.7g |Protein 2.7g

Caribbean BBQ Sauce

Preparation Time: 10 minutes
Cooking Time: 10 minutes
Serves: 12

Ingredients:

- 1 tsp. vegetable oil
- 3 slices bacon, diced
- 1 medium onion, finely chopped
- 1 cup tomato sauce
- ½ cup black rum
- 1 lemon, juiced
- ⅓ cup brown sugar
- 1 dash chili sauce

Preparation:

1. In a medium pan, heat the vegetable oil, bacon, and onion over medium-high heat. Cook until the bacon is evenly browned and the onions are soft.
2. Reduce the heat to low and stir in the tomato sauce and rum with the bacon and onion in the pan. Cook the mixture for roughly 2 minutes on low heat.
3. Combine the lemon juice, brown sugar, and chili sauce in a mixing bowl. Add to the pan and simmer for another 8 minutes.

Serving Suggestion: Serve with any main dish.

Variation Tip: Add spices

Nutritional Information per Serving:

Calories 91kcal | Fat 3.6g | Sodium 0.16g | Carbohydrates 9g | Fiber 0.9g | Sugar 7.1g | Protein 1.3

Frozen Cranberry Sauce

Preparation Time: 5 minutes
Cooking Time: 15 minutes
Servings: 26

Ingredients:

2 (12 oz.) packages frozen cranberries
⅔ cup white sugar
⅔ cup firmly packed brown sugar
½ cup orange juice
1 tbsp. lemon juice
⅛ tsp. ground cinnamon
1 tbsp. vanilla extract

Preparation:

1. In a 2- to 3-quart saucepan over high heat, bring the cranberries, white sugar, brown sugar, orange juice, lemon juice, and cinnamon to a simmer. Simmer for 8 to 10 minutes, uncovered, stirring periodically, until the cranberries are soft when poked.
2. Remove from the heat and set aside for 10 to 15 minutes to allow the vanilla extract to infuse. Serve immediately or refrigerate for up to 1 week in an airtight jar.

Serving Suggestion: Serve with bread.

Variation Tip: You can use it on cakes or sugar cookies.

Nutritional Information per Serving:
Calories 57kcal | Fat 14.8g | Sodium 0g | Carbohydrates 14.1g | Fiber 1.2g | Sugar 12.2g | Protein .2g

Ranch Snack Mix

Preparation Time: 10 minutes
Cooking Time: 15 minutes
Servings: 24

Ingredients:

- 4 cups crispy corn and rice cereal
- 2½ cups small pretzels
- 2½ cups cheese-flavored crackers (optional)
- 2 cups oyster crackers
- ½ cup peanuts (optional)
- ⅔ cup vegetable oil
- 1 (1 oz.) package ranch dressing mix
- ¼ tsp. garlic powder

Preparation:

1. Preheat the oven to 275°F.
2. Combine the cereal, pretzels, cheese-flavored crackers, oyster crackers, and peanuts in a larg mixing bowl.
3. In a small bowl, combine the vegetable oil, ranch dressing mix, and garlic powder. Pour over th cereal mixture and toss to combine. Place on a large baking sheet to cool.
4. Bake until toasted and fragrant in a preheated oven, stirring gently halfway through.

Serving Suggestion: Serve with dips.

Variation Tip: Nothing, it's perfect as it is!

Nutritional Information per Serving:
Calories 197kcal | Fat 11g | Sodium 0.51g | Carbohydrates 21.3g | Fiber 1g | Sugar 1g | Protein 3.3

Game Day Crunch

Preparation Time: 10 minutes
Cooking Time: 10 minutes
Serves: 20

Ingredients:

- 1 cup brown sugar
- ½ cup butter
- ¼ cup white corn syrup
- 1 tsp. baking soda
- ½ tsp. vanilla extract
- 6 cups crispy wheat cereal squares (such as Wheat Chex®)
- 2 cups pretzel sticks
- 1½ cups peanuts

Preparation:

1. In a large microwave-safe bowl, combine the brown sugar, butter, and corn syrup. Microwave on high for 3½ minutes, or until bubbling. Microwave for another 2 minutes after stirring.
2. In a large mixing bowl, combine the brown sugar, baking soda, and vanilla extract.
3. Toss the cereal squares, pretzel sticks, and peanuts in the brown sugar mixture until thoroughly covered. Cook the mixture for 2 minutes in the microwave. Stir thoroughly and microwave for another minute.
4. Spread the mixture onto waxed paper and cool completely; break into small pieces.

Serving Suggestion: Serve as an evening snack

Variation Tip: Add vanilla or strawberry essence to enhance the flavor.

Nutritional Information per Serving:
Calories 210kcal | Carbohydrates 27g | Protein 4g | Fat 10g | Fiber 2g | Sugar 14g | Sodium 0.40g

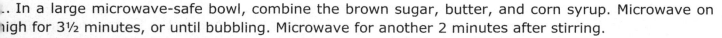

Caramel Popcorn

Cooking Time: 30 minutes
Preparation Time: 1 hour
Serves: 20

Ingredients:

- 1 cup butter
- 2 cups brown sugar
- ½ cup corn syrup
- 1 tsp. salt
- ½ tsp. baking soda
- 1 tsp. vanilla extract
- 5 quarts popped popcorn

Preparation:

1. Preheat the oven to 250°F. The popcorn should be placed in a very large bowl.
2. Melt the butter in a medium saucepan over medium heat.
3. Combine the brown sugar, corn syrup, and salt in a mixing bowl. Add to the butter and bring to a boil, continually stirring. Boil for 4 minutes without stirring.
4. Remove from the heat and whisk in the baking soda and vanilla extract.
5. Pour a thin stream over the popcorn and toss to coat.
6. Transfer to 2 big shallow baking pans and bake for 1 hour in a preheated oven, stirring every 15 minutes. Remove from the oven and set aside to cool fully before serving.

Serving Suggestion: Serve as a movie-time snack.

Variation Tip: Drizzle chocolate syrup over the popcorn and enjoy!

Nutritional Information per Serving:
Calories 253kcal | Fat 14g | Sodium 0.33g | Carbohydrates 34g | Sugar 22g | Fiber 1g | Protein 0.9g

Spring Salad

Preparation Time: 10 minutes
Cooking Time: 12 to 15 minutes
Servings: 8

Ingredients:

12 slices bacon
2 heads fresh broccoli, florets only
1 cup celery, chopped
½ cup green onions, chopped
1 cup seedless green grapes
1 cup seedless red grapes
½ cup raisins
½ cup blanched slivered almonds
1 cup mayonnaise
1 tbsp. white wine vinegar
¼ cup white sugar

Preparation:

. Cook the bacon in a large deep pan over medium-high heat until uniformly browned.
. Drain, crumble, and place on a plate.
. Toss the bacon, broccoli, celery, green onions, green grapes, red grapes, raisins, and almonds in a large salad dish.
. Combine the mayonnaise, vinegar, and sugar in a mixing bowl. Toss the salad in the dressing to coat it.

Serving Suggestion: Serve after it has been refrigerated to cool.

Variation Tip: Sprinkle dried fruits and nuts over the dish.

Nutritional Information per Serving:
Calories 540kcal | Carbohydrates 28.9g | Protein 9.4g | Fat 15g | Sodium 0.54g | Fiber 4g | Sugar 2g

Broccoli Salad

Preparation Time: 15 minutes
Cooking time: 12 to 15 minutes
Servings: 8

Ingredients:

- 1 lb. bacon
- 4 cups broccoli florets
- 5 green onions, chopped
- ¼ cup sunflower seeds
- ¼ cup golden raisins
- 1 cup mayonnaise
- ½ cup white sugar
- 6 tbsp. red wine vinegar

Preparation:

1. In a large skillet, cook the bacon over medium-high heat until uniformly browned. Allow the bacon to cool before crumbling and setting aside.
2. Toss the broccoli, green onions, sunflower seeds, raisins, and bacon in a large mixing bowl.
3. Combine the mayonnaise, sugar, and red wine vinegar in a small bowl. Toss the veggies in the dressing to coat them. Cover and chill until ready to serve.

Serving Suggestion: Serve chilled.

Variation Tip: Add almonds.

Nutritional Information per Serving:
Calories 542kcal | Carbohydrates 23g | Protein 8.4g | Fat 47g | Sodium 0.64g | Fiber 1.4g | Suga 17g

Enchilada Sauce

Preparation Time: 10 minutes
Cooking time: 30 minutes
Serves: 12

Ingredients:

- 1 tbsp. vegetable oil
- 1 cup onion, diced
- 3 tbsp. garlic, chopped
- 1 tsp. dried oregano
- 1 tsp. ground cumin
- ¼ tsp. ground cinnamon
- 3 tbsp. all-purpose flour
- 5 tbsp. hot chili powder
- 4½ cups chicken broth
- ½ (1 oz.) square semisweet chocolate

Preparation:

1. In a large saucepan, heat the oil over medium-high heat. Add the onion and cook until it is soft. Sauté for a few minutes after adding the garlic, oregano, cumin, and cinnamon.
2. Stir in the flour and chili powder until the sauce has thickened. Reduce the sauce until it reaches the appropriate consistency by slowly whisking in the chicken broth.
3. Stir in the chocolate until it has melted and is evenly distributed.

Serving Suggestion: Serve it with enchiladas.

Variation Tip: Add more spices.

Nutritional Information per Serving:
Calories 43kcal| Carbohydrates 6.1g | Protein 1g | Fat 2.2g | Sodium 0.03g | Fiber 1g | Sugar 2g

Pineapple Lemonade

Preparation Time: 20 minutes
Cooking time: 5 minutes
Servings: 6

Ingredients:

- ½ cup sugar
- 1 cup lemon juice
- 1 cup pineapple juice
- 2 tbsp. lime juice

Preparation:

1. To prepare the simple syrup, melt the sugar in a medium saucepan with 1 cup water over medium heat, stirring constantly, until the sugar dissolves; set aside to cool.
2. Whisk together the simple syrup, lemon juice, pineapple juice, lime juice, and 5 cups of water in a big pitcher. Refrigerate until completely cold.

Serving Suggestion: Serve over ice.

Variation Tip: Add sugar and salt according to your taste.

Nutritional Information per Serving:
Calories 97kcal | Fat 0.2g | Sodium 1g | Carbohydrates 25g | Sugar 22g | Protein 0.3g | Fiber 0.3g

Watermelon Slush

Preparation Time: 5 minutes
Cooking Time: 5 minutes
Serves: 4

Ingredients:

- 5 cups diced seedless watermelon
- 2 tbsp. sugar
- Juice of 1 lime, optional

Preparation:

1. Puree the watermelon, sugar, lime juice, and 1 cup ice in a blender until smooth.
2. Serve right away.

Serving Suggestion: Serve with ice.

Variation Tip: Add sugar and salt according to your taste.

Nutritional Information per Serving:
Calories 48kcal | Fat 0.7g | Sodium 0g | Carbohydrates 11g | Fiber 1g | Sugar 10g |Protein 1g

Raspberry Peach Prosecco Punch

Preparation Time: 5 minutes
Cooking time: 5 minutes
Serves: 10

Ingredients:

- 12 oz. frozen raspberries
- 2 cups peach nectar, chilled
- 1 bottle prosecco, chilled
- Ice cubes

Preparation:

1. Fill a big glass pitcher or dispenser halfway with the frozen raspberries. Finish with a drizzle of peach nectar and a splash of prosecco.
2. Fill the remaining ice cubes in the pitcher or dispenser. Serve chilled after stirring.

Serving Suggestion: Serve with ice.

Variation Tip: You can add sugar and salt according to your taste.

Nutritional Information per Serving:

Calories 45kcal | Fat 1g | Sodium 0g | Carbohydrates 11g | Fiber 3g | Sugar 8g | Protein 1g

Blueberry Lemonade

Preparation Time: 20 minutes
Cooking time: 5 minutes
Serves: 6

Ingredients:

- ½ cup extra-fine granulated sugar
- 1 cup blueberries
- ¾ cup freshly squeezed lemon juice

Preparation:

1. To prepare the blueberry simple syrup, melt the sugar in 1 cup of water in a medium saucepan over medium heat, stirring constantly. Bring to a boil, then reduce to a low heat and simmer for 3 to 4 minutes, or until the blueberries have broken down.
2. Allow to cool after straining the blueberry mixture through a cheesecloth or a fine sieve.
3. Combine the blueberry simple syrup, lemon juice, and 5 cups of water in a large pitcher. Refrigerate until completely cold.

Serving Suggestion: Serve over ice and frozen blueberries, if desired.

Variation Tip: You can add sugar and salt according to your taste.

Nutritional Information per Serving:
Calories 101kcal | Fat 0g | Sodium 0g | Carbohydrates 25g | Fiber 1.5g | Sugar 24g | Protein 0g

White Sangria Sparkler

Preparation:: 5 minutes
Cooking Time: 5 minutes
Serves: 6

Ingredients:

- 1 apple, sliced
- 1 orange, sliced
- 1 bottle Chardonnay (Mirassou)
- ½ cup orange juice
- 1 can club soda or Sprite or diet Sprite
- ½ cup cranberries, fresh or dried
- 2 sprigs rosemary, for garnish
- 2 tbsp. granulated sugar, for garnish
- 2 tbsp. water, for garnish

Preparation:

1. Combine the apple, orange, orange juice, cranberries, and Mirassou Chardonnay in a large pitcher.
2. Stir in the club soda (or Sprite) in the pitcher.
3. Wet the rosemary and roll it in granulated sugar. Allow time for drying.
4. Fill a glass halfway with sangria and top with rosemary.

Serving Suggestion: Serve with ice if desired.

Variation Tip: For toppings, you can add more fruits.

Nutritional Information per Serving:
Calories 39kcal | Carbohydrates 10g | Protein 1g | Fat 1g | Saturated Fat 1g | Sodium 0g | Fiber 2g Sugar 7g

Berry Sangria

Preparation Time: 5 minutes
Cooking time: 5 minutes
Serves:8

Ingredients:

- 1 bottle rosé wine
- 1 cup strawberries, thinly sliced
- ½ cup raspberries
- ½ cup blackberries
- ½ cup blueberries
- ¼ cup sugar
- 12 oz. lemon-lime soda (optional)

Preparation:

1. Combine the rosé wine, strawberries, raspberries, blackberries, blueberries, and sugar in a big pitcher.
2. Allow for at least 1 hour of chilling time in the refrigerator.

Serving Suggestion: Serve over ice with lemon-lime soda.

Variation Tip: You can add sugar and salt according to your taste.

Nutritional Information per Serving:
Calories 131kcal | Fat 0.1g | Sodium 0.01g | Carbohydrates 17g | Fiber 2g | Sugar 14g | Protein 0.5g

Strawberry Pineapple Mimosas

Preparation Time: 5 minutes
Cooking Time: 5 minutes
Serves: 8

Ingredients:

- 1½ cups orange juice
- 1½ cups pineapple juice
- 1 bottle sparkling white wine, chilled
- ½ cup strawberries, thinly sliced

Preparation:

1. Combine the orange and pineapple juice in a pitcher.
2. Fill champagne glasses halfway with the orange-pineapple combination.
3. Pour the white wine into the glasses and serve immediately.

Serving Suggestion: Serve with ice.

Variation Tip: Garnish with strawberries, if desired.

Nutritional Information per Serving:
Calories 124kcal | Fat 0.1g | Sodium 0g | Carbohydrates 13g | Fiber 0.5g | Sugar 10g | Protein 0.5g

Sparkling Cherry Lemonade

Preparation Time: 15 minutes
Cooking Time: 15 minutes
Serves: 6

Ingredients:

- 2 oz. cherries, pitted
- ¾ cup freshly squeezed lemon juice
- ⅔ cup sugar
- 4 cups sparkling water

Preparation:

1. Blend the cherries, lemon juice, and sugar until smooth to produce the cherry syrup. Refrigerate until completely cold.

Serving Suggestion: Serve over ice and sparkling water.

Variation Tip: You can add sugar and salt according to your taste.

Nutritional Information per Serving:

Calories 23kcal | Fat 0g | Sodium 0.02g | Carbohydrates 6g | Fiber 0g | Sugar 6g | Protein 0g

Warming Ginger Soda

Preparation Time: 5 minutes
Cooking time: 5 minutes
Serves: 6

Ingredients:

- 11 oz. unpeeled fresh root ginger, finely sliced
- 8 oz. caster sugar
- 6 cloves
- 1½ lemons, zest and juice
- 1-pint cold water
- 1¾ pint soda water

Preparation:

1. Put the ginger, sugar, cloves, lemon zest, and lemon juice in a pan.
2. Cover with the cold water and heat over medium-low heat to slowly dissolve the sugar.
3. Increase the heat and cook for 10 minutes.
4. Strain the mixture through a fine sieve into a large jug.
5. Allow the drink to cool before topping up with the soda water.

Serving Suggestion: Serve with fresh mint leaves as a garnish.

Variation Tip: Let the mixture sit in the refrigerator for a few days for the flavors to infuse.

Nutritional Information per Serving:
Calories 105kcal | Fat 0g | Sodium 0g | Carbohydrates 38g | Fiber 0g | Sugar 38g | Protein 0g

Apple Cider Vinegar Tonic

Preparation Time: 5 minutes
Cooking Time: 5 minutes
Serves: 1

Ingredients:

- 1 cup brewed green tea, chilled
- 1 tbsp. raw cider vinegar
- 1 tsp. pure maple syrup
- 1 tsp. fresh ginger, grated
- 1 lemon wedge (optional)

Preparation:

. Stir the tea, vinegar, syrup, and ginger in a medium glass.

Serving Suggestion: Serve with ice and a squeeze of lemon, if desired.

Variation Tip: Add sugar and salt according to your taste.

Nutritional Information per Serving:

Calories 22kcal | Fat 0.1g | Sodium 0g | Carbohydrates 5g | Fiber 4g | Sugar 14g | Protein 0g

Zucchini Cupcakes

Preparation Time: 10 minutes
Cooking Time: 27 minutes
Serves: 6

Ingredients:

- 3 large eggs
- 1⅓ cups sugar
- ½ cup canola oil
- 1 tsp. salt
- ½ cup orange juice
- 2 tsp. baking powder
- 1 tsp. almonds, sliced
- 2½ cups all-purpose flour
- 2 tsp. ground cinnamon
- 1 tsp. baking soda
- ½ tsp. ground cloves
- 1½ cups zucchini, shredded

For the frosting:

- ½ cup margarine, cubed
- ¼ cup 2% milk
- 1 tsp. vanilla extract
- 1½ to 2 cups confectioners' sugar
- 1 cup brown sugar

Preparation:

1. Preheat the oven to 350°F. Combine the first five Ingredients in a mixing bowl.
2. Mix together the dry Ingredients; gradually add to the egg mixture and combine well. Toss in the zucchini.
3. Fill 66% of the way up of paper cupcake liners in a cupcake tray. Bake for 20 to 25 minutes, then cool on a wire rack for 10 minutes.
4. In a large pan, combine the brown sugar, margarine, and milk for the frosting. Over medium heat, bring to a boil; cook and stir. Remove from the heat and mix in the vanilla. Cool to room temperature.
5. Gradually beat in the confectioners' sugar until the frosting is smooth. Ice the cupcakes with the frosting cupcakes.

Serving Suggestion: Serve with tea.

Variation Tip: Add sugar according to your taste.

Nutritional Information per Serving:
Calories 214kcal | Fat 5.1g | Sodium 0.23g | Carbohydrates 31g | Fiber 5g | Sugar 2.1g | Protein 17

Crusty Fruit-Filled Treat

Preparation Time: 10 minutes
Cooking Time: 20 minutes
Serves: 6

Ingredients:

- ½ cup sugar
- ½ cup brown sugar
- 3 tbsp. all-purpose flour
- 1 tsp. ground cinnamon
- ¼ tsp. ground ginger
- ¼ tsp. ground nutmeg
- 7 cups tart apples, sliced
- 1 tbsp. lemon juice
- 2 ready-made pie crusts
- 1 tbsp. butter
- 1 large egg white
- Additional sugar

Preparation:

1. Preheat the oven to 375°F.
2. Combine the sugars, flour, and flavoring in a large bowl. Store in an airtight container until use.
3. Toss the apples with the lemon juice in a suitable-sized dish. Add the sugar-flour mixture and toss to cover the apples.
4. Fill a 9-inch pie pan with 1 layer of pie crust and trim the borders. Fill with the apple mixture, then top with butter. Roll out the remaining crust to fit the top of the pie. The edges should be trimmed, sealed, and fluted.
5. Whisk the egg white until it is foamy, then pour it over the outer layer. Sprinkle sugar on top.
6. Place in the oven and bake for 20 minutes or until the crust is golden brown and the filling is bubbling. Allow to cool on a wire rack.

Serving Suggestion: Cut into slices and serve with tea and sliced strawberries.

Variation Tip: Add sugar according to your taste.

Nutritional Information per Serving:
Calories 212kcal | Fat 12g | Sodium 0.32g | Carbohydrates 4.4g | Fiber 4.4g | Sugar 8g | Protein 17.3g

Winning Apple Crisp

Preparation Time: 10 minutes
Cooking Time: 65 minutes
Serves: 6

Ingredients:

- 1 cup all-purpose flour
- ¾ cup rolled oats
- 1 cup stuffed brown sugar
- 1 tsp. ground cinnamon
- ½ cup butter, softened
- 4 cups apples, chopped

Preparation:

1. Preheat your oven to 350°F.
2. Combine the first four Ingredients in a suitable bowl.
3. Cut in the butter until the mixture is crunchy.
4. Press half of the mixture into a greased 2½ -quart baking dish or a 9-inch square baking dish
Spread the apples on top.
5. Combine the sugar, cornstarch, water, and vanilla in a small saucepan. Bring to a boil; simmer and
stir for 2 minutes, or until thick and clear. Pour the liquid over the fruit. Sprinkle with the rest of the
crunch mixture.
6. Bake for 60 to 65 minutes or until the apples are soft.

Serving Suggestion: Serve warm with frozen yogurt.

Variation Tip: Add sugar according to your taste

Nutritional Information per Serving:
Calories 197kcal | Fat 15g | Sodium 0.20g | Carbohydrates 58.5g | Fiber 4g | Sugar 1g | Protein 7.3g

Sweet Fritters

Preparation Time: 10 minutes
Cooking Time: 5 minutes
Serves: 4

Ingredients:

Oil for frying
2½ cups all-purpose flour
1 tsp. baking powder
1 tsp. baking soda
1 pinch salt
1 cup milk
⅝ cup sweetened condensed milk

Preparation:

1. In a deep fryer, heat the oil to 350°F.
2. In a mixing bowl, whisk together the baking powder, baking soda, salt, and flour with the milk and condensed milk until smooth.
3. With the assistance of a spoon, drop the batter into the oil. Deep fry until golden brown, about 3 to 4 minutes.

Serving Suggestion: Serve with the fritters warm with an assortment of fresh berries.

Variation Tip: Add sugar according to your taste.

Nutritional Information per Serving:
Calories 450kcal | Fat 11g | Sodium 0.56g | Carbohydrates 87.8g | Fiber 2.1g | Sugar 29.1g | Protein 3.9g

Dutch Apple Cake

Preparation Time: 10 minutes
Cooking Time: 1 hour 30 minutes
Serves: 8

Ingredients:

- 3 medium tart apples, peeled and diced
- 1 cup and 3 tbsp. sugar
- 1 tsp. ground cinnamon
- $2/3$ cup margarine, softened
- 4 large eggs, whisked
- 1 tsp. vanilla extract
- 2 cups all-purpose flour
- $1/8$ tsp. salt

Preparation:

1. Preheat the oven to 300°F.
2. Combine the apples, 3 tablespoons of sugar, and cinnamon in a bowl; set aside for 60 minutes.
3. In a separate bowl, cream together the margarine and the remaining sugar until light and fluffy. Add 1 egg at a time and beat until incorporated. Pour in the vanilla extract.
4. Combine the flour and salt; gradually add to the beaten mixture and beat until smooth.
5. Fill a greased 9 x 5-inch baking tin halfway with the mixture.
6. Place the apple mixture on top.
7. Bake for 1½ hours. Cool for 10 minutes before transferring from the tin to a wire rack.

Serving Suggestion: Serve with your favorite hot beverage.

Variation Tip: Add sugar according to your taste.

Nutritional Information per Serving:
Calories 253kcal | Fat 8.9g | Sodium 0.34g | Carbohydrates 24.7g | Fiber 1.2g | Sugar 11.3g | Protein 5.3g

Funnel Cake

Preparation Time: 25 minutes
Cooking Time: 30 minutes
Serves: 12

Ingredients:

- 1 cup water
- ½ cup butter
- ⅛ tsp. salt
- 1 cup all-purpose flour
- 4 eggs
- 2 tbsp. powdered sugar

Preparation:

1. Preheat the oven to 400°F and line a baking sheet with parchment paper.
2. Bring the water, butter, and salt to a boil in a medium pan.
3. Add the flour and whisk vigorously until the mixture forms a ball.
4. Allow the mixture to cool for 10 minutes before adding one egg at a time and beating thoroughly with a wooden spoon.
5. Place the dough in a big plastic bag and snip a ¼ to ½ inch hole in one corner of the bag with scissors.
6. Pipe the dough into twelve 3 to 4-inch circles (funnel-shaped) on the prepared baking sheet.
7. Bake for 20 minutes before transferring to a wire rack to cool. While the cake is still warm, dust powdered sugar over it.
8. Ready to serve!

Serving Suggestion: Serve with tea.

Variation Tip: Add some cinnamon to the mixture before baking.

Nutritional Information per Serving:
Calories 135kcal | Fat 9.4g | Sodium 0.10g | Carbohydrates 9.3g | Fiber 0.3g | Sugar 1.4g | Protein 3.3g

Dole Whip

Preparation Time: 5 minutes
Cooking Time: 30 minutes to chill
Serves: 2

Ingredients:

- 4 oz. pineapple juice
- 1 big scoop vanilla ice cream
- 2 cups frozen pineapple chunks
- 2 tbsp. sugar
- Splash of lemon juice
- A pinch of salt

Preparation:

1. In a blender, combine all of the Ingredients and blend until a smooth and creamy concoction emerges. Toss in the pineapple chunks.
2. Freeze the mixture for 30 minutes, then use a piping bag to swirl the mixture into dessert glasses.

Serving Suggestion: Serve immediately.

Variation Tip: Use different juices or fruits if you wish.

Nutritional Information per Serving:
Calories 261kcal | Fat 3g | Sodium 0.04g | Carbohydrates 53g | Fiber 3g | Sugar 44g | Protein 3g

Buttermilk Pancakes

Preparation Time: 5 minutes
Cooking Time: 8 minutes
Serves: 8

Ingredients:

- 1¼ cups of all-purpose flour
- 1 tsp. baking soda
- 1 tsp. baking powder
- 1¼ cups granulated sugar
- 1 pinch salt
- 1 egg
- 1¼ cups buttermilk
- ¼ cup cooking oil

Preparation:

1. While making the batter, preheat the pan by keeping it on medium heat.
2. Blend all of the dry Ingredients together in a mixing bowl.
3. Blend all of the wet Ingredients together in another large mixing bowl.
4. Carefully mix the dry Ingredients into the wet Ingredients until they are completely combined.
5. In a pan, melt some butter.
6. Pour the batter onto the pan slowly until you have a 5-inch circle.
7. When the pancake edges appear to have solidified, flip it, and cook the other side.
8. Steps 6 to 7 should be repeated until the batter is finished.

Serving Suggestion: Serve with a dollop of melted butter and a drizzle of maple syrup.

Variation Tip: Add some blueberries to the batter mix.

Nutritional Information per Serving:
Calories 118kcal | Fat 5.7g | Sodium 0.12g | Carbohydrates 7g | Fiber 0.1g | Sugar 0.3g | Protein 4.9g

Mango Popsicles

Preparation Time: 5 minutes
Cooking Time: 0 minutes
Serves: 6

Ingredients:

- 1 large mango, peeled and diced
- 1 large ripe banana, peeled and sliced
- Juice of 1 lime
- ½ cup canned coconut milk

Preparation:

1. In a blender, combine all of the Ingredients and mix until smooth.
2. Fill popsicle molds with the mixture, insert a wooden stick, and freeze for at least 6 hours or until solid.

Serving Suggestion: Serve just as they are!

Variation Tip: Add a little sugar according to your taste.

Nutritional Information per Serving:
Calories 63kcal | Fat 4g | Sodium 0g | Carbohydrates 8g | Fiber 1g | Sugar 6g | Protein 1g

Chocolate Covered Bananas

Preparation Time: 10 minutes
Freezing Time: 2 hours
Serves: 12

Ingredients:

- 4 large ripe bananas, peeled and each cut into 3
- ¾ cup semisweet chocolate chips, melted
- ¼ cup shredded coconut

Preparation:

1. Line a baking sheet with wax paper.
2. Place a popsicle stick in each banana cube and then top with the melted chocolate and a sprinkling of coconut.
3. Place the banana popsicles on the baking sheet and freeze for about 2 hours, or until they are completely frozen.

Serving Suggestion: Serve immediately.

Variation Tip: Instead of shredded coconut, you can use chopped nuts.

Nutritional Information per Serving:
Calories 100kcal | Fat 4g | Sodium 0g | Carbohydrates 18g | Fiber 1.9g | Sugar 6g | Protein 1g

Four Weeks Meal Plan

Week 1

	BREAKFAST	DRINK	LUNCH	SNACK	DINNER
Day 1	Banana Egg Pancakes	Pineapple Lemonade	Pot Chicken Tenders Green Salad	Ranch Snack Mix	Spicy Vegetable Stew With Coconut Fresh Herb Salad
Day 2	Egg Muffins	Raspberry Peach Prosecco Punch	Grilled Chicken Breast Fresh Herb Salad	Game Day Crunch	Mushroom Buckwheat Risotto
Day 3	Chickpea Flour Pancakes	Blueberry Lemonade	Creamy Garlic Chicken	Caramel Popcorn	Balsamic Lentil Pies With Vegetable Mash
Day 4	Omelet	White Sangria Sparkler	Lemon Butter Chicken	Zucchini Cupcakes	Sweet Potato Parcel Fresh Herb Salad
Day 5	Egg With Avocado Bread	Berry Sangria	Parmesan Chicken Cutlets	Crusty Fruit-Filled Treat	Chickpea Fajitas Caribbean BBQ Sauce
Day 6	Breakfast Potato	Strawberry Pineapple Mimosas	Apricot Glazed Chicken Spring Salad	Winning Apple Crisp	Spinach, Sweet Potatoes, and Lentil Dhal
Day 7	Avocado Sandwich	Sparkling Cherry Lemonade	Chicken Fried Rice Broccoli Salad	Sweet Fritters	Butternut Chili

Week 2

	BREAKFAST	DRINK	LUNCH	SNACK	DINNER
Day 1	Tomato Mozzarella Bread	Apple Cider Vinegar Tonic	Honey Sesame Chicken	Zucchini Cupcakes	Salmon With Chia Seeds, Fennel Slaw, and Pickled Onions
Day 2	Tempeh Sandwich	Raspberry Peach Prosecco Punch	Chicken Enchiladas	Caramel Popcorn	Moroccan Salmon
Day 3	Scrambled Egg With Cheese	Sparkling Cherry Lemonade	Mexican Chicken Soup Spring Salad	Winning Apple Crisp	Brazilian Fish Stew
Day 4	Banana Egg Pancakes	Strawberry Pineapple Mimosas	Lobster Bisque Broccoli Salad	Dutch Apple Cake	Baja Taco Bowl
Day 5	Egg Muffins	Berry Sangria	Slow-cooked Italian Pulled Pork	Dole Whip	Pan-Seared Steelhead Trout
Day 6	Chickpea Flour Pancakes	White Sangria Sparkler	White Miso Black Cod	Mango Popsicles	Baked Haddock With Tomato and Fennel
Day 7	Omelet	Blueberry Lemonade	Portuguese Fish Stew	Chocolate Covered Banana	Slow Cooked Lamb Shanks

Week 3

	BREAKFAST	DRINK	LUNCH	SNACK	DINNER
Day 1	Egg With Avocado Bread	Watermelon Slush	Beef Massaman Thai Curry	Funnel Cake	Oven-Baked Meatballs
Day 2	Breakfast Potato	Berry Sangria	Beef and Broccoli Stir Fry	Winning Apple Crisp	Braised Pork in Sweet Soy Sauce
Day 3	Avocado Sandwich	Warming Ginger Soda	Beef Stroganoff	Dole Whip	Pot Chicken Tenders
Day 4	Tomato Mozzarella Bread	Pineapple Lemonade	Italian Beef Stew	Chocolate Covered Banana	Grilled Chicken Breast
Day 5	Tempeh Sandwich	Strawberry Pineapple Mimosa	Mexican Chicken Soup	Mango Popsicles	Creamy Garlic Chicken
Day 6	Scrambled Egg With Cheese	Berry Sangria	Beef Brisket Soup	Buttermilk Pancakes	Lemon Butter Chicken
Day 7	Banana Egg Pancakes	White Sangria Sparkler	Meatloaf	Game Day Crunch	Parmesan Chicken Cutlets

Week 4

	BREAKFAST	DRINK	LUNCH	SNACK	DINNER
Day 1	Egg With Avocado Bread	Berry Sangria	Parmesan Chicken Cutlets	Crusty Fruit-Filled Treat	Chickpea Fajitas
Day 2	Breakfast Potato	Strawberry Pineapple Mimosas	Beef Brisket Soup	Wining Apple Crisp	Spinach, Sweet Potatoes, and Lentil Dhal
Day 3	Chickpea Flour Pancakes	White Sangria Sparkler	White Miso Black Cod	Mango Popsicles	Baked Haddock With Tomato and Fennel
Day 4	Omelet	Blueberry Lemonade	Portuguese Fish Stew	Chocolate Covered Banana	Slow-Cooked Lamb Shanks
Day 5	Scrambled Egg With Cheese	Berry Sangria	Beef Brisket Soup	Buttermilk Pancakes	Lemon Butter Chicken
Day 6	Banana Egg Pancakes	Strawberry Pineapple Mimosa	Meatloaf	Dole Whip	Parmesan Chicken Cutlets
Day 7	Scrambled Egg With Cheese	Sparkling Cherry Lemonade	Mexican Chicken Soup Spring Salad	Winning Apple Crisp	Brazilian Fish Stew

Conclusion

Macro diets emphasize counting the number of macronutrients consumed rather than the number of calories. People require substantial amounts of macronutrients in their diet. These nutrients help provide the energy needed for the body to function and stay healthy. The three primary macronutrients are proteins, lipids, and carbohydrates. These are essential for a variety of physiological processes.

Some people may benefit from keeping track of their macro consumption to achieve their health and fitness objectives. Counting macros, however, can be time-consuming and limiting for some people. While keeping track of macro consumption has its advantages, it also has its drawbacks. Before beginning a macro diet, it is a good idea to consult with a doctor or a nutritionist.

Made in the USA
Coppell, TX
16 December 2022

89501775R00052